the LIMERICK BOOK

HINKLER
BOOKS

The Limerick Book
First published in 2003 by Hinkler Books Pty Ltd
17-23 Redwood Drive
Dingley VIC 3172 Australia
www.hinklerbooks.com

© Hinkler Books Pty Ltd 2003

ISBN 1741 2116 54

Cover designer: Sam Grimmer
Editor: Kristin Odijk
Typesetting: Midland Typesetters, Maryborough, Vic, Australia
Printed and bound in Australia

CONTENTS

INTRODUCTION

We hope you enjoy this edition
Of words and erudition
Honouring the Limerick
Which does the trick
Of monitoring the Human Condition.

There is something beautiful about the limerick. I think it is its rhythm, one of the most natural sequences of beats known to humankind. I'm sure if it was researched, you would find that the two-long-lines/two-short-lines/one-long-line sequence is inserted in our biological make-up from the day we are born. People pick up on it very quickly, and it stays with them forever.

Say the word 'limerick' among any group of people and someone is certain to start sprouting one. It may be corny or silly, beautifully constructed or downright rude, but the rhythm will be perfect. Add the pertinent fact that the last words of lines 1, 2 and 5 rhyme, as do lines 3 and 4, but with a separate sound, all done in about 29 words, and you have a thing of exquisite literary beauty. This is why it is worth preserving old limericks and generating new ones – as this book does.

It is believed that the limerick started to appear around 1820, and that the name comes from the Irish town of the same name, and a song that began 'Will you come up to Limerick?'

In this book we publish two sets of poems – '16 Stories of Women' and '15 Stories of Men' – that appeared in London in 1820 and are among the first pieces that could be described as limericks. We also have contributions by the man who, 25 years later, turned the original limerick style into an art form. His name was Edward Lear, and he led a remarkable life, among other things illustrating works of John Gould, the famous bird expert.

Lear wrote more than 100 limericks, produced in two books in 1846 and 1855, although he preferred to call them 'Nonsense.' Each limerick came with one of his own masterful illustrations, and they proved immediately popular and enduring.

Lear's original 'Nonsense' poems are featured in this book. After reading a few, it will dawn on the first-time reader that there is a subtle but significant difference between Lear's pieces and what we know as a limerick today. That is, Lear's fifth line is merely a repeat or a slight variation of the first line – invariably, the final word in the first and fifth lines is the same. These days, of course, the fifth line has become the punch line, with a new rhyming word providing the 'twist', a concept that began to develop a few years after Lear set the benchmark. Of course, the other significant difference is the content – Lear talked about men with birds nesting in their beards and ladies with their shoes untied.

Over the years the limerick began to rapidly evolve into a social parody, a political manifest, and a comment on the heroes, villains and events of the times. Fart jokes became popular, too! But all the while the little limerick began to further dip its toe into the uncharted waters of romance. Which inevitably led to sex . . . Poor old Edward would turn in his grave if he knew what his beloved 'Nonsense' poems have turned into.

While the 21st-century limerick is still used as a technique for putting down the boss, pointing out the inadequacies of politicians, deflating egos, telling crazy tales and, yes, spreading rip-roaring fart gags, for some people there is only one formula, and that is: The limerick = Sex.

The sex aspect started as far back as the late 19th century and took off from there, becoming the everyday vehicle for amazing tales about men and women with grossly enlarged genitalia, bizarre sexual practices and an insatiable appetite for all things crass.

In this book we cover all of these areas, with the book being split into major components. We honour the works of Edward Lear and the early writers. We look at the myriad of classic limericks that have endured over the years. We explore new material, now available on the Web, and from many diverse sources, and we contribute many originals that we have written ourselves. But also, we compre-hensively cover the large and ever-expanding area of sex, the almost customary form of limerick as we know it today.

Each chapter is divided into subgroups for easier reading. Along the way, you will come across limericks in different sections that sound very similar. That is because they have been amended or updated over the years, and embraced by a new generation, so it is worth noting the change, however subtle.

Indeed, stretching down the years from Edward Lears's Old Man of the South, 'who had an immoderate mouth', to the search for a connection between the mouth of George Bush and a brain, the limerick has provided us with a wonderfully accessible and enjoyable commentary on life throughout the ages. So, here's to that limerick rhythm, that starts Da da-da, da da-da, da da-da, and gets into your brain. It's a beautiful thing.

GRAEME JOHNSTONE

NEW, ORIGINAL LIMERICKS

The limerick provides a great opportunity to amuse and intrigue. It can be witty, funny, crazy. It can comment on events or just amuse. Here's our contribution to the world of limericks, with a selection of new and fresh originals that we have written ourselves.

GRAEME JOHNSTONE
ELSIE AGNES ALLEN

Just for Fun . . .

A hungry cannibal named Joan
Ordered takeaway up on the phone
'I'll have baked explorer
And a great white snorer
And roasted missionary on the bone . . .'

I do want to Save the Whale
Its treatment is beyond the pale
But when I think of a cause
Something makes me pause
And go back to the bar for an ale . . .

He was my ultimate health guru
He gave me a diet and exercise to do
'Til I awoke one morning
The dreadful truth dawning
He'd died. He was mortal, too . . .

My good mate Barry the Bomb
Dropped a stinker of a fart with aplomb
It's of such magnificence
And great significance
It's been released on CD-ROM . . .

A pompous explorer named Katter
About his travels, loved to chatter
But through misadventures
He'd loosened both dentures
And when Katter would natter, he'd clatter . . .

Our vicar, a pulpit denouncer
Ran off to become a nightclub announcer
But his DJ-ing technique
Made the dancers all freak
So now he's a liturgical bouncer . . .

Whoops!

I went to the kickboxing master
To learn to be a fleet-footed blaster
But my kick to his knackers
Sent him quite crackers
And the rest of the course was a disaster.

There was an innocent young knave
Who found his way into a cave
The poor boy took flight
Into the dark of the night
He had stumbled on an ecstasy rave . . .

Wearing a cape at the top of a hill
I jumped off, for a bit of a thrill
I floated on the breeze
With the greatest of ease
And landed in northern Brazil . . .

A hippie from outback Australia
Hit the city in his finest regalia
But his rainbow braces
Brought scorn to their faces
They regarded his regalia a failure.

A rather hungry Sheik
Took his fishing rod down the lake
He threw his line in
With a worm and a pin
And pulled out two pieces of flake . . .

New Technology

I was tapping away on the keyboard
When suddenly I said 'Oh, Lord.'
There was a frightening flash
Another big crash!
I'm putting this PC to the sword.

Our boss, the IT guru, Cyrus
About computers tried to inspire us
His enthusiasm palled
And the project stalled
When the system succumbed to a virus.

My odd computer mate, Mac
On a PC would go clackety-clack
I said, 'Mac, with your name
Surely an Apple's the game.'
So he hurled his PC out of his shack.

I once had a clever young suitor
Whose mind was just like a computer
When I caused her to crash
On the strength of a pash
A flick of her switch would reboot her.

                              – Simon Hobbs

Changes

Poor Frank was unhappy and mean
He was always making a scene
But after an op
He's feeling tip-top
You see, Frank is now Francine . . .

A dispirited bloke named Ray
Shifted to San Francisco Bay
'It's hard to prove
But here I move
And suddenly I'm happy and gay . . .'

A very unhappy girl named Ann
Decided on a new life's plan
They re-did her plumbing
She came out humming
Now Ann is Stan the Man . . .

There was a young man named Jason
Every morning he'd put his new face on
Rouge and red lippy
A dress that was hippy
It was hard to get a ticket at the station . . .

A young big buck named Dangles
Saw the world from different angles
He felt real strange
So he made the change
Now he wears cute dresses and bangles.

Travel

A seasoned traveller named Bernie
Chose Rome for a wonderful journey
But the computer went silly
And sent him to Chile
Now Bernie is seeking an attorney.

A first-class passenger, Lord Heerage
Made his liner friends aware of his peerage
But at cards he went funny
Gambled away all his money
And had to sail home in steerage . . .

I'd like to travel to Ghana
And eat a nice banana
But I won't roam
I'll stay at home
It's the ticket money I can't garner . . .

A Person Named . . .

An annoying fellow named Niall
Had a smarmy patronising smile
He snorted some coke
And ended up broke
That wiped the grin from his dial.

A match-wielding guy named Gyro
Turned into a methodical pyro
He burnt London down
And half Sydney town
And a generous portion of Cairo.

A demure young lady named Eloise
Began each day with a big sneeze
In clusters they'd come
At the rise of the sun.
Causing one helluva breeze!

A nice little fellow named John
Had trouble getting his trousers on
His braces would twirl
And get in a whirl
His helpful sisters were often called upon.

There was a young bloke named Herman
Who hated the sight of vermin
'I dislike mice and rats,
And ants and bats,
I reckon they are the worst type of cur, man ...'

A baby boomer named Graeme
Went to the disco to slay 'em
But he caused a kerfuffle
Doing his sideways shuffle
And only caused dance-floor mayhem.

Laurie, the man from Wiaawera
Would give you a drink just to cheer ya,
He'd offer a beer
To give you good cheer
Click glasses and say, 'Well, here's to ya.'

Alan the Silent from Swan Reach
Would practice what he did preach
Think before you speak
Don't be a stickybeak
Now, there's some rules we could teach.

Kathleen was a farmer's wife
She stood by him through trouble and strife
In flood and in drought
Year in and year out
She was loyal and true all her life.

There was a man named Fred
Who never had a thought in his head
When he tried to muster
His braincell cluster
They all would hop back into bed . . .

Graeme, philosopher and poet,
Could read anything and instinctively know it
At quiz shows he was able
To help win for his table
Which made others unhappy, though they tried not to
    show it.

Elsie is a right regular tart
She is earthy, but has a kind heart
But 'tho she's the brain
No-one went to the pain
Of thanking her for all of the things in which she took
    part.

Elsie makes sure things get done
Tho' that's still not enough for some
Behind the tough exterior
Is a soft interior
As she marches to the beat of her own drum.

There was a young girl named Georgina
My, you should have seen 'er
She was about six foot two
Weighed three hundred and two
Round our way, there was nobody meaner.

There was a young lady named Mary
Who made herself up as a fairy
Then at 12.15
She would turn all green
And this fairy would look rather scary.

The Drink

There was a young man from Buchan
Who was known for his standard of chuckin'
He would drink and drink
Then run to the sink
And shout, 'This is better than f . . f . . f . . . feeling sick . . .'

There was a man named Carter
Who needed a morning heart starter
A glass of beer
Gave him good cheer
But didn't make all that much smarter . . .

Poor Michael Seamus McGinn
Spent too much time on the gin
He got into strife
Lost his poor wife
And is now looking pale and thin.

A bloke named Wally McHandy
Loved a drop of the brandy
But the hit to his liver
Started to make him shiver
So now he has just a small shandy.

Diets

The Fat Boy down by the lake
Would eat cake after cake after cake
The doc said 'Stop,
Your heart will go plop.'
Now he's Diet Boy, as thin as a rake . . .

The diet-conscious Francine
Was slimmer than a Lima bean
When Francine walked by
In the twink of an eye
She was gone before she was seen . . .

There was a young man from Highett
Who went on a punishing diet
But he confided one day
If he had his way
He'd grab a pork chop and fry it . . .

Massive & Mighty

There once was a girl named Aphrodite
Whose boobs were massive and mighty
Her waist was quite thin
And so was her chin
But she had to wear a Size 48 nightie . . .

There was a young girl named Whipple
Who had one big enormous nipple
To boost the other
She got her mother
To enhance it with a 3D stipple . . .

The girl with the world's biggest chest
Had boobs that were the absolute best
But after a 10 metre walk
And a bit of a talk
She'd have to sit down and rest . . .

A busty pop-singer from Colditz
Had Germany's largest pair of titz
She went on TV
Popped out, you see
And they were her two biggest hitz . . .

A lady had such monstrous boobs
They hung well past her pubes
To lift them both back
She made up a rack
Of pulleys, and cogs, and tubes . . .

Sport

There once was a premier jockey
About his diet he became rather cocky
He could ride no faster
From gorging on pasta
And stuffing himself with gnocchi.

There was a wild child named Dennis
Boy was he one hell of a menace
Then luckily one day
A coach passed his way
Now he's World Number One in Tennis.

My lying friend Robert the Huge
Claimed he could ride the luge
Halfway down the valley
He landed on his belly
And that ended his subterfuge.

A bloke who supported St Kilda
Left his wife, a Bomber fan named Hilda
'If she said one more word
About dear little James Hird
I reckon I would have bloody near killed her . . .'

Sampras, the Grand Slam Pete
Turned tennis into a treat
He won so many games
They expanded his names
Pete, Re-Pete and Three-Pete.

What a ridiculous game is cricket
Such a long time between each wicket
For hours you stare
In the sun and the glare
You can take your cricket and stick it.

Cricket is a gentleman's game
We play for joy, not fame
It's love, not war
We aim for a draw
After five days everything's the same . . .

Is there ever a game that is more borin'
Than watching an old codger snorin'
'Wake up, Hector
You're the Chief Selector
And I think another wicket is fallin' . . .'

An Aussie leg-spinner named Shane
Took a pill to stop his weight gain
'I want to be thin,
Get rid of my chin.'
He got a year to add to his pain.

A great spin bowler named Warne
Took a pill and caused a storm
He blamed one other
To whit, his mother
Which left him wide open to scorn.

What a crazy race is the Grand Prix
Cars flash by, one, two, three
But as they close the park
From daylight to dark
How much is this costing you and me?

That bald bloke Michel Klim
Does he know how to swim!
With that windmill style
He wins by a mile
A speedboat can't catch up to him.

The Winter Olympics story is told
Of how Steve Bradbury won gold
At the final bell
The others all fell
And Braddles came in from the cold.

A skijumper, Eddie the Eagle
Jumped like a low-flying beagle
So the Olympic fold
Put him out in the cold
And declared the Eagle illegal.

Eric the Eel from Equatorial Guinea
Was small and dark and skinny
He swum like a stone
And finished all alone
But was the hero of the Games at Sydney.

To the uninitiated it would seem
The prime purpose of a football team
Is to get sloshed on Saturday
Attract chicks every other day
And fulfil every young man's dream . . .

The ref from hell would give a decision
That would spark outraged derision
His whistle he'd blow
For what? Who'd know?
What he needed was a brain circumcision.

A soccer played named McLeaper
Fancied himself as a keeper
But he ran into the poles
And let in too many goals
So now he's the dressingroom sweeper . . .

A keen football player named Brick
Marked, and for the goal he did kick
The Grand Final depended
Poor Brick was upended
And back over his head it did flick.

A football hero named Wayne
Couldn't control all things with his brain
A bathroom meet
Turned up the heat
And he's Adelaide-bound on the train.

Life could never be more bumpy
For the poor old football umpy
We yell with derision
At each decision
No wonder he's down in the dumpy . . .

Cathy Freeman like the wind she can run
She's that type that thinks running is fun
At the Sydney Olympics
She silenced her critics
She ran so fast she nearly hit the ton.

There was a great runner from Mackay
Who like the wind she could fly
When she won a great race
The aboriginal flag she would place
Around her shoulders and make it fly high.

Australians love tennis and Lleyton
When he gets beaten we find it deflatin'
But when he smashes his opponents
Cuts their games to components
We love it! We find it breath takin'.

Ian Thorpe has huge hands and huge feets
It's handy when at his swim meets
He dives into the water
Goes faster than he oughter
And all his competitors defeats . . .

Her serves and volleys blister
You simply cannot resist her
Leave the court
Your score is nought
You've been walloped by a Williams sister.

I'm Serena, and she's Venus
There's very little between us
We both play great
And the titles rotate
We're tennis talent in the extremus . . .

The beads bounce all over the court
And no matter how hard you'd fought
They served a slam
They volleyed a wham
Venus and Serena rule the sport.

Golf, your heart it does break
The mis-hits and bad shots you make
My enthusiasm palls
I only hit two good balls
In the bunker, when I stood on the rake . . .

There was once a golfer with a stutter
Whose career ended up in the gutter
He could hit a beautiful iron
And his drives were inspirin'
But he could never come to grips with the
 p . . . p . . . p . . . putter . . .

A rugby union player named Crumb
Put his head down and went in the scrum
The pack was so tight
In the showers that night
He found a set of dentures up his bum.

A classy athlete named Brian
Took up American gridiron
He didn't mind the padding
Or the bruise-resistant cladding
But in that hot helmet his brains were fryin'.

I went and saw a game of soccer
It turned out to be quite a shocker
The game was all right
It was the post-match fight
When the fans went right off their rocker!

Disasters

There was once a bottled-up genie
Who was really a bit of a meanie
If you wished for a hat
He'd say 'Take that.'
And all you'd get was a beanie!

Poor Jacko could only drive a nail
With the pace and speed of a snail
You'd guarantee by gum
He'd hit his thumb
And shout 'Jeezus Christ' without fail.

Instead of doing the stitchin'
Twin girls would dance in the kitchen
Hours of rock and roll
Would take their toll
And spark a scene of kitchen friction . . .

Wobbly Bits

A rather well-hung old geezer
Inadvertently stuck his dick in the freezer
It was so chilly
It shrank his big willy
To find it, he now needs a tweezer . . .

There was once a bloke named Cropper
Boy, did he have a whopper
It was so damned large
He carried it on a barge
With a sign reading: 'Beware of me flopper . . .'

A South American gaucho named Billy
Had definitely the world's longest willy
On a very good day
It stretched all the way
From the top to the bottom of Chile.

A well-endowed man named Klinger
Had the world's most gi-normous dinger
When he pulled it out
His new love would shout
'Klinger, that dinger's a zinger . . .'

Big Dick had the world's longest penis
It stretched from Sydney to Venus
He waved it in the air
Shoved it everywhere
What Dick did with that penis was heinous.

A bloke with longest of dicks
Could do some fabulous tricks
Conduct a choir
And put out a fire
While balancing three hundred bricks.

A Greek-Egyptian named Spiro
Had a dick as thin as a biro
Made from soft plastic
It was so elastic
That it stretched from Athens to Cairo.

There was a young man named McCoodle
Who had the world's largest doodle
But to keep it in trim
And hanging well on him
It took commitment, exercise and boodle

A sexually frustrated groover
Sought solace with the nozzle of a Hoover
The mechanical blow-job
Didn't half make him sob
'Cos it took off the tip of his doover . . .

A thrill-seeking chap named Phil
Was really a bit of a dill
Thinking it was nice
He put his dick on ice
And all he got was a chill.

Ivan Stravinsky Skavar
Had the biggest cock in the world by far
Such was its strain
When he went by train
It travelled in its own separate car . . .

A giant of a man from Mt Hutts
Had by far the world's biggest guts
It was as big as a barge
But if you think that's large
You should've seen the size of his nuts.

There was a wild man from Calcutta
Who was really a bit of nutter
He wore pink lace
And tattoos on his face
And bathed his balls in the gutter.

There was a man named Schlonger
With a long and pointy old donger
With a little attention
To fire prevention
He could use it as a barbecue pronger . . .

Robbers

A would-be thief named Frank
Devised a plan to rob a big bank
He failed to remain calm
Touched off the alarm
Now the lock to his cell goes 'clank . . .'

A latter-day Robin Hood
Tried to do the people some good
But they said, 'That's okay,
We get the dole each Thursday.'
Disillusioned, he went back to the wood.

I wanted to be a hob-nobber
And wear their nice sort of clobber
To be that flash
I needed the cash
So I became a professional bank robber . . .

Environment

I suppose I should really protest
To save the birds in the nest
But it's such a pain
To go marching in rain
I think I'll just lie down and rest.

Hot Love

There was a couple willing and able
To make love on a rickety table
Three legs caved in
She grazed her chin
And his condition is given as 'stable' . . .

There once was a bloke from Bermuda
Who flew with a girl on Garuda
After a big glass of brandy
He got rather randy
Took her to the loo and screwed her . . .

There was a boy from Cadiz
Whose love life had little fizz
Whenever he tried
He dried up inside
And couldn't go on with the biz . . .

There was a girl with a glorious chasm
Who had never had an orgasm
She knew all the facts
To reach a climax
But all she got was a spasm ...

At a Paris café I met Jean-Paul Forlore
Who whispered to me 'Je t'adore.'
In that place
To our disgrace
We did it there right on the floor ...

Religious

A curious girl named Estelle
Came across an abandoned well
She peered over the rim
A flaming hand pulled her in
And she now lives forever in Hell.

A holier-than-thou chap named Bevan
Avoids the deadly sins seven
His language is clean
His soul is pristine
For his sake we hope there's a Heaven ...

I want to hear the heavenly choir
As the angels sing higher and higher
At least that is my hope
But if they give me too much rope
I might end up down below by the fire . . .

Events

On Jesse Martin, the youngest person to sail solo around the world:
Round the globe Jesse Martin did sail
His little boat refused to fail
Some said he was lucky
But he was really quite plucky
Surviving critics, tornado, and gale . . .

On Lou Richards, a '40s and '50s star of Australian Rules football, and media megastar:
For Lou Richards it's been an 80-year trip
Even now he's cool and he's hip
After footy gave way
He began to parlay
His career into Louie the Lip . . .

On the finding of the body of a lonely old woman in her own home, who had died two years earlier:
Elsie Brown died two years ago
That she was dead no-one did know
She always hid her face
Stayed in 'My Space'
And that's the way she wanted to go . . .

Eighty-two-year-old Elsie Brown
Was dead two years before her bones were found
Not because no-one cared
Just because no-one dared
To enter dear Elsie's sacred ground.

On Neven Solian, a Melbourne trivia genius, whose extraordinary skills rankle with opponents and quiz-organizers alike:
Neven Solian is no trivia fool
Read, revise, remember is his rule
He's banned from quiz nights
To give lesser lights
Their chance to scoop the pool . . .

About a World War 2 war hero who died in his 90s:
Phil Rhoden was a hero bright
He led his troops when might was right
On the Kokoda Track
He turned the Japanese back
And the Aussies won a crucial fight.

*About Adam Gilchrist 'walking' after he had been given
'not out' by the umpire in the World Cup.*
The mighty wicketkeeper Gilly
Walked, and critics said he was silly
But it was good to hear
Someone so sincere
Saying he couldn't bat on willy-nilly.

Fads

Psychoanalysts study secrets of the mind
Things that motivate, ties that bind
But none of 'em agree
So how can we?
Just understand each other and humankind.

I read my astrology stars each day
They tell me whether to go or to stay
What's my agenda?
I'm a pretender
I go and do what I what, anyway . . .

Politics

As a politician, he's very nifty
Conservative and shrewd and thrifty
But at the end of the day
Johnny's led us the way
Back to around nineteen fifty . . .

Despite many people's pleas
The government stopped the refugees
Their aim was specific
Spread them around the Pacific
And win the election with ease.

The government loves the sensation
Of being an interfering nation
Telling others overseas
"Do it this was, please."
What about our own welfare and education?

Simon, the next of the Creans
Is not passionate enough in what he means
If he stays so droll
He'll lose every poll
And han more votes to the Greens

Churchill enjoyed a good war
He made it his own personal score
But as soon as it was over
The people rolled over
And showed old Winston the door.

Harold Holt promised LBJ
The Aussies would go with him all of the way
But an afternoon swim
Proved rather grim
Poor old Harry just floated away . . .

LBJ had a slow-drawling tongue
And a war in a place far-flung
Truly, he'd put each guest
To the ultimate test
By showing how well he was hung.

President Nixon, Richard Milhouse,
Watergate, he tried to douse
But the *Washington Post*
Continued the roast
And got him out of the White House.

Just who did kill JFK
Is debated still to this day
Surely some of the toll
Came from the grassy knoll
Despite what the Warren Commission had to say.

Not even a novelist could be the hatcher
Of the character called Margaret Thatcher
It was a powerful den
Run by Attila the Hen
And for ten years, no-one could catch her.

Jimmy Carter, all smiling and fair
Dared enter the Washington lair
But they said he was nuts
Kicked him in the guts
All because he showed he did care.

Was there a duller President than Ford?
He certainly pulled no-one's rip-cord
The thing that was scary
Was that good old Gerry
Was there 'cos Nixon fell on his sword.

Ronald Reagan was a movie star
Then, how did he get so far?
To be the Prez
Perhaps it's what you sez
Rather than how you think, what you know, and
    who you are . . .

First, there was Bush the older
He just got bolder and bolder
He loved to bark
At poor old Iraq
But the voters gave him the cold shoulder.

They say Clinton had a high IQ
He loved to think, and act, and do
But sometime's he'd stray
Look the other way
And say 'Hello, girls, how do you do . . .?'

Bob Hawke was red in the face
We'd won a big-time yacht race
'If you must go to work,
You're boss is a jerk,
And the company's a bloody disgrace . . .'

Paul Keating never would yield
Deflected criticism with a tough shield
But to this day
We still have to play
On that bloody annoying level field.

Fraser was the Lord of Nareen
A sterner PM never to be seen
He was ruthless and tough
And called Gough's bluff
But these days he's caring and green . . .

McMahon the big-eared Billy
Had a voice that was tinny and chilly
He was the master
Of the Lib's poll disaster
In the end it was all a bit silly.

Dear old John Grey Gorton
Really shouldn't have ought'n
Given his vote
To Billy the Goat
That's what you get for being sportin'.

Menzies, known better as Ming
Was a lumbering old conservative thing
He loved Royalty and torts
And Lording the Cinque Ports
And the power that politics could bring.

'Men and women of Australia,' said Gough
Ending years of rule by the toff
But the shocked big noters
Ignored the voters
They conspired, and said 'Gough, piss off . . .'

Big Malcolm from Melbourne town,
Went around in his dressing gown.
When asked, 'Why so dressed?'
He replied when pressed.
'I don't wish to be caught with my pants down!'

There was a Colt from Kooyong
Who would be PM 'fore too long
Then one day
It all fell away
The colt found Johnny a bit too strong.

Pauline made them run for cover
They said she was dumb like no other
To their shock
She developed a flock
So she was put into court by Big Brother.

Kirsty Marshall was a ski jumper
Gold on the slopes would pump her
But her baby on the breast
Put the House to the test
And some old buggers tried to dump her . . .

War

The trouble with George W. Bush
Is that he keeps on opening that moosh
It's a second-rate brain
Running at full strain
It's a time someone said to him 'Shoosh!'

George is obsessed with the Axis of Evil
He says, 'They do the work of the d-e-evil
'Let's drop a big bomb
We're right, they're wrong
And the oil is ours for retrieval . . .'

On a large flat TV screen
The war from Iraq can be seen
The coalition of willing
Find it so thrilling
But the rest of us find it obscene.

George says he'll slay the terrorism beast
And hold a celebratory feast
But there's more in store
Unless he goes to the core
And brings peace to the Middle East

Bin Laden, he hid in a cave
Avoiding a very close shave
The Yanks opened the can
Bombed Afghanistan
From Pakistan, Osama gave 'em a wave . . .
The so-called coalition of the willing
Would go to war for just one shilling
Howard and Blair
Bush and his stare
Lock up the enemy and give them a grilling.

When the war drums were beating
The investors, they were retreating
They got out of the shares
It was the time of the bears
The paper value was rapidly depleting.

But when the rockets started to fly
The stock market went high
The bulls charged
Their portfolios enlarged
It's sadistic and leaves you to cry.

When signing the oil with East Timor
Alex the Downer demanded more
'Don't make a fuss
Just give it to us
Make us rich, and bugger the poor . . .'

Fanatics, their wills they would see
Impressed on all those who disagree
Within their dominion
They respect no-one's opinion.
We see it each night on TV.

There's no denying Saddam Hussein
Ruthlessly inflicts a lot of pain
But we won't solve the problem
By simply just bombing them
And leaving kids' bodies in the lane.

We marched to Parliament's door
We walked 'til our feet were raw
But our leaders who abhor us
Chose to simply ignore us
And continued with their bloody Gulf war.

We marched until our feet were sore
We arrived at Parliament's door
A young girl's call
On her T-shirt said it all
It said: 'Make Chocolate, Not War'.

There once was a leader named Blair
Very proud of his thatch of hair
But his passion for war
Caused a furore
And soon he was thinning up there.

You wonder about our politicians
And their love of guns and munitions
They declare war
Hide behind the door
And let the innocent suffer their decisions.

Have you ever seen a grimmer sight
Than missiles hitting Baghdad at night?
It's a bloody disgrace
But with a po-face
George says it's all for 'peace' and 'what's right'.

The war drums were beating loud
But Old Europe stood out from the crowd
'They need a good push,'
Said George W. Bush
At least they hold their head up proud.

There are no breaks to the TV transmission
It's all there in stereo colour vision
But this is not cricket
It's the war of the wicked
George's bombers on a cruel mission.

Jacques Chirac opposed the war
Not convinced of what they're fighting for
He said that France
Would prefer the chance
For Iraq's weapons to be laid on the floor.

Much to their anger and regret
There's an aspect our leaders did forget
They can't spin us a line
About the Gulf this time
The truth about this war's on the Net.

Beware the doctors of spin
Who say what's out and what's in
They manipulate news
And mould your views
Surely that is the Original Sin.

Rumsfeld cites the Convention
Of not giving POWs attention
But for him it's okay
At Guantanamo Bay
To hold people in disgraceful detention.

To the tune of 'London's Burning':
Baghdad's burning
Baghdad's burning
War is looming, bombs are booming
Children crying, leaders lying
Baghdad's burning
For peace we're yearning

Pets

Madge our lovely white cat
Is big and fluffy and fat
She idles the day
Between rest, eat and play
And you can't do much better than that!

A little Aussie Terrier named Appleby
Was the most impossible rascal you'd ever see
Would he come at your bidding?
Obey? Are you kidding?
Appleby just wanted to be what he wanted to be.

A dog exhibitor named Roe
About her canines she'd crow
When asked how she'd gone
She'd reply with aplomb
'No doubt, best bitch in show ...'

I once went to West Pakistan
And brought home an orang-utan
My wife took the kids
My life hit the skids
And the neighbours, they all off and ran.

Farts & Other Eruptions

There was a successful grocer named Bart
Who sold baked beans from a cart
Among his sales techniques
He used to bare both cheeks
And let off a gi-normous fart.

There once was a bloke named Martin
The epitome of all great fartin'
He would, quite readily
Emit a 'Silent but Deadly'
And the crowd would soon be departin'.

Once, I had a great-uncle
On his nose he had a huge carbuncle
It grew and grew
'Til it weighed six stone two
And was bigger than an elephant's trunkle . . .

Isn't it terrible how a nice dimple
Can disappear under a red pimple?
That nasty eruption
Can cause such disruption
And temporarily make you look simple.

The truth about old Wyatt Earp
He actually killed people with a burp
He didn't fire his gun

Just let off a big one
'It's the vibration that gets 'em,' he'd chirp.

My uncle was always a tease
Between each word he'd let off a sneeze
As he'd go for the hanky
It'd get people cranky
But he thought it was a helluva wheeze.

My cousin Buckminster Grott
Had a nose brimming with snot
'Be careful,' we'd say
'Don't turn the wrong way
He'll sneeze, and you'll cop the lot.'

A big German lady Renata
Became the world's greatest farter
When she let one go
The whole neighbourhood would know
Seismologists were sent in to chart her.

I tried for a Bachelor of Arts
I thought I had lots of smarts
But my only trip
Is to let one rip
So they gave me a Master of Farts.

An aspiring entertainer named Hing
Unfortunately could not really sing
So in between scenes
He ate all his beans
And farted God Save the King!

Places

An aspiring politician from Blain
Was born with only half a brain
Against all direction
He went for election
And was voted in, again, and again . . .

There was a young man from Wonthaggi
Whose pants were particularly baggy
The cloth on his seat
Went down to his feet
So he gave them away to a swaggie.

There was an old fellow from Bourke
Who hated the thought of hard work
He'd do his best
To knock off and rest
He knew every anti-work lurk.

There was a young lad from the Lakes
Who had a terrible case of the shakes
From wine and brandy
The occasional shandy
And Jack Daniels on his Corn Flakes . . .

There was a young girl from Rye
Born with a turn in her eye
While we were conversin'
Her eye was reversin'
I couldn't concentrate as hard as I'd try.

Alan the artist from Highett
Teaching, he thought he would try it
But the kids ran amok
Alan went into shock
And his brain they nearly did fry it.

An ardent young lover from Omeo
Thought himself quite a Romeo
He started to flirt
Put his hand up her skirt
Now Romeo is home all aloneo . . .

German Jorge kept order atop Lakes hill
He was affable and kind until
The boys would be boys
And make too much noise
One firm boot and they're rolling still.

An Irish priest who lived in Lakes
Told his congregation 'I've all it takes
To exorcise devils
Who live in the rebels
After that, we'll have tea and cakes . . .'

There was a family from Bendigo
Who thought they were the only ones in the know
To everyone's irritation
They hogged the conversation
The room, it would empty just so . . .

A little old lady from Bairnsdale
Appeared to be sickly and frail
But given the chance
She'd get up and dance
Her arms and her legs she would flail.

A wily old wizard from Deepdene
Was the greatest magician to be seen
When things got tough
He'd disappear in a puff
Of partly vaporised steam.

Two ballroom dancers from Moe
Were slick, and smooth, and showy
They slipped on the floor
And slid out the door
That's what happens when you get too toey . . .

There was a young man from Sale
Who delighted in the odd ale
But alas one night
He got into a fight
Now, he's trying to scratch up the bail.

Food

At School Food Technology
We tried a leek soup recipe
Something went wrong
It started to pong
Instead of leek, it tasted more like pee . . .

A devil-may-care restaurant cook
Made a mess of cooking a chook
His boss, said 'See,
Use this recipe.'
Now the cook cooks the chook by the book . . .

There was a young man named Calvacho
Who hated hot soup, tho' he was macho
He dared to be bold
And made it cold
And found he'd invented gazpacho.

There was a boy who like to scoff pasta
He'd keep eating it faster and faster
One day he hit the wall
He couldn't even crawl
It was a faster pasta disaster.

A mum had a daughter named Shelley
Who started to grow big in the belly
'What's this?' said Mum
Patting Shelley's tum
'You've spent too much time down the Deli . . .'

A young girl with eyes of blue
Wanted to make some Irish stew
But her talent in the kitchen
Was not what you'd call bitchin'
And it tasted like industrial-strength glue.

There was a young man named Jeff
Who yearned to be a good chef
But instead of cutting out gristle
He could blow a good whistle
So they turned him into a ref . . .

Great Moments

It was a moment not be missed
He held the prize in his fist
The Melbourne Cup
The Governor General stands up
And gee, he's just a little bit pissed ...

It was indeed a wonderful sight
Orville and Wilbur Wright
Walking the walk
At old Kittyhawk
And taking our world into flight.

They say that man stood on the Moon
On an amazing July afternoon
But I'm no believer
I think some deceiver
Has tricked us with a video cartoon ...

They said that it would never fall
It was concrete, rigid and tall
The people said 'Enough!'
And showed they were tough
By knocking down the old Berlin Wall.

Occupations

There was once a veteran plumber
Who refused to dig ditches in summer
'Now that I'm older
I only dig when it's colder
Digging dirt in the heat is a bummer . . .'

There was once a ballet dancer
Renowned as a vigorous prancer
But to his great despair
He wasn't very big 'down there'
So he put in some socks as an enhancer.

There was a forgetful gardener named Keith
Who lost both sets of his teeth
Two kindly old coppers
Searched for the choppers
And found 'em at the bottom of the Heath.

There was once a painter named Barty
Who went to his opening night party
He ate all his greens
Then some baked beans
And became the ultimate arty-farty . . .

An untidy orthodontist named Mac
Kept his dentures in one great stack
When passing train'd rumble
The dentures would tumble
And all would go clackety-clack.

There once was an ambitious politician
To become PM was his main mission
He got caught in the vibe
Accepted a bribe
Putting paid to his big ambition . . .

A meteorologist named O'Kane
Travelled through sunny old Spain
He brandished some sticks
Did two magic tricks
And made it rain on the plain . . .

A tradesman had an enormous great rear
His bum-crack was the size of a pier
It was such a design
Someone tacked on a sign
Saying: 'Park your bicycle here . . .'

To be a yachtsman you must have the power
To cop a drenching, hour after hour
Mucking around in boats
Is like tearing up big dollar notes
While standing under a cold shower . . .

There was a musician named Mace
Who plugged in his electrical bass
The wire it was damp
And blew up the amp
He plays somewhere now in outer Space . . .

A General will die in his bed
Not a drop of his blood will he shed
For a soldier it's no fun
He dies by the gun
It makes a pacifist like me see red . . .

Maria was a wonderful gel
That worked at night as a bar-belle
She'd be warm and funny
But if you paid her no money
She could turn your life into hell . . .

Bored personal assistant Beryl
And tired chartered accountant Cheryl
Decided to be free
Set up house in a tree
Cheryl and Beryl have really gone feral . . .

A religious young lady named Proctor
Became a theological doctor
But all the church men
Pulled together again
On spurious grounds they defrocked her.

A timber-cutter named Jim
Went very far out on a limb
He cut on the wrong side
Went for the long ride
Ended in hospital pale and grim.

A sailor who loved a cigarette
Lit one up beneath the poop-deck
The flame caught the fuel
Went whoosh! It was cruel
The old ship became a floating wreck.

There was a man who read statistics
He'd go on and on about logistics
When asked to speak
He'd bore the meek
And reduce the mild to tantistrics.

There once was a clever tailor
Who made a suit for a sailor
'I've made the coat-tail
In the shape of a pail
So if the boat floods, you can bail 'er.'

The man who sells real estate
Is delivered the world on a plate
He doesn't own the property
He auctions off regularly
But still gets his cut, gee thanks mate!

The pizza delivery man,
Set off with the pie in his hand
He encountered an Alsatian
Who ate him and his creation
And left a few bones in the sand.

Anything you want written, he can write
The wordsmith works day and night
He pens a good word
The smart, the absurd
It's true, the pen has the might.

How I Wish . . .

There's something for which I strive
While I'm still fit and alive
That's to sing and dance
Crack jokes and prance
And become Number 6 in Hi-5.

I wish I had been on 'Get Smart'
Delivering funny lines at the start
On the shoe-phone line
Chatting to 99
And the cone of silence, now that was an art.

My life is one depressing niggle
There's nothing that makes me giggle
I sit in my room
Overcome with gloom
Oh, how I wish I was a Wiggle . . .

How I wish that I was a Wiggle
I could jump and sing and jiggle
The kids would play
And shout hooray
And my bank balance would keep getting biggle ...

How I dream of playing guitar
And being a rock 'n' roll star
But my boss each day
Says, 'Hey, you, hey, hey!
Keeping rolling that road with tar ...!'

How I wished I'd have played the fool
And danced and sung and been cool
There would have been nothing neater
Than to appear with Benita
And John on morning 'Playschool'.

Ned

Australia's favourite son, Ned Kelly
Was born with fire in his belly
The law brought him to heel
Despite plates of steel
And the shoot-out made news on the telly ...

The Kelly legend won't stagger
He was a hero, a killer, a bragger
But one telling of the tale
Beyond the pale
Was the movie starring Mick Jagger ...

Imperfections

There was a young man from Crete
Who was born with two left feet
When he danced the Zorba
It was quite an absorber
To watch him miss the main beat ...

There was a man named De Vere
Who was sadly missing one ear
He'd miss the plot
And not say a lot
Until you asked: 'Would you like a beer ...?'

There was a silvertail named Keith
Who was 'full of it' up to his teeth
He suffered delusions
And was so full of illusions
That when he left the room, what a relief!

I have to say my mind just boggles
At the site of my mate's new goggles
To tie them on
He has to rely upon
A series of pulleys and ratchets and toggles.

Music

Michael Jackson says that he grows
As natural as a blossoming rose
But under the urgin'
Of his plastic surgeon
He's lost the plot with his nose ...

Madonna is one on her own
She even put her boobs in a cone
She sings and dances
Acts and prances
And takes everything into a new zone.

Judy, Keith, Athol and Bruce
When will you finally cut loose?
It's a bottomless well
The Seekers' Farewell
For God's sake, call it a truce ...

They waved the magic music wand
Over a bloke called Plastique Bertrand
He sang 'Ca Va Pour Moi'
For bar after bar
It was a hit all over du monde.

The Stones have a singer named Jagger
Around the stage he does swagger
He still sings pop
But perhaps he should stop
Before it turns to a stagger . . .

A band called the Rolling Stones
Spawned dozens and dozens of clones
But they kept touring along
Singing song after song
Much to the next generation's groans.

A musician named Brian Jones
Got sacked from the Rolling Stones
He could play guitar
But not swim very far
So he never did make old bones.

The Beach Boys sang about sun
And surfing and water and fun
But of the horde
Who could ride a board
The drummer was the only one.

The fabulous Elton John
As a musician, he is the Don
But when he gets prissy
And throws a big hissy
They say: 'Elton, keep your wig on . . .'

Man, Elton was the singer I dug
Until he went into a mental fug
He stormed off the stage
In a hell of a rage
Was that a bug under his rug?

The wildest band was The Who
A loud and colourful crew
They played at full pace
Then smashed up the place
And the music was pretty good, too . . .

The Who's drummer Keith Moon
Was also a professional loon
His kit he smashed
His cars he crashed
And then he came to the end of the tune.

The Who had a drummer named Moon
Boy, he was a helluva loon
He went at full throttle
Including the bottle
That's why he left us too soon.

Ozzy, the Prince of the Drastic
Was pure heavy metal fantastic
He ate a bat's head
For dinner and said
'Bugger, I thought it was plastic ...'

George, John, Ringo and Paul
Formed the biggest band of them all
It got too exciting
They started fighting
So Paul ran off down the hall ...

An act that'd be hard to follow
Your pride you'd just have to swallow
It's got a great beat
And turns up the heat
It's the Ina-Gada-Davida drum solo ...

Jail

There was a persistent jail escapee
Who was approximately seven foot three
Each morning he tried
To run off and hide
They always had him back in by Tea.

A prisoner went over the wall
Hurt himself in the terrible fall
But he didn't care
He ran like a hare
And was last seen entering Nepal . . .

A car thief named Lightfingers MacKenzie
Was jailed by the judge in a frenzy
His Honour went mad
And said Mac was bad
Because he'd nicked the old bugger's Benzie . . .

My brother had an extra-strong bevvie
And tried to scarper with a Chevy
He was so pissed
Forward gear he missed
The judge came down on him rather heavy.

Did you hear about Patrick McGill?
He swallowed a jagged little pill
He turned rather pale
Spent two nights in jail
Which took the edge off the thrill.

A well-to-do thief named McGint
Thought he'd retire after robbing the Mint
Alas, he did fail
They whacked him in jail
And for the rest of his life he'll be skint.

A nasty bastard name Jewell
Challenged his foe to a duel
He fired his gun
And shot him in one
Now Jewell is doing time on cold gruel.

A mild accountant named Drubbs
Use to swindle companies and clubs
He went overboard
Spent up like lord
He's doing seven in Wormwood Scrubs . . .

Movies

A flatulent movie-goer named Lind
His farts he would never rescind
But one matinee
He just flew away
Apparently he'd Gone With The Wind . . .

A fly-weight boxer named Cocky
Modelled himself on Rocky
But all he could see
Was his opponent's knee
So now little Cocky's a jockey.

This week I began to ponder
About which film I was feeling quite fonder
Not Gump or Chicago
Or Shaft or Key Largo
For me it's A Fish Called Wanda.

It's quite a film *Forrest Gump*
His girlfriend lives in a dump
His mum is feckless
His buddy is legless
There's a stump, and a hump and a jump.

I went to see Lord of the Rings
To see what thrills that it brings
Talk about Two Towers
Sit on your butt for hours!
Both arms and one leg are in slings.

Kiwis

Why are there so many Kiwis in Australia?
I personally put it down to the failure
Of our own litigation
To enforce limitation
On the number allowed to sail 'ere . . .

It's a point of intriguing fascination
Being discussed throughout the nation
If you just sit down
And look around
There's always a Kiwi in any situation ...

Medical

A woman named by the name of McCole
Had a rather distinguishing mole
The doctor said 'Dot,'
'That's one hell of a spot.
It's bigger than the Superbowl ...'

A young lunatic named Deuteronomy
Was in need of a frontal lobotomy
But sadly my friend
They did the wrong end
And came out with a total colostomy ...

A medical student named Sydney
Donated to science a kidney
That left him with one
Which wasn't much fun
He had to go on dialysis, didn't he ...?

A doctor's patient named Klapp
Felt so bound up she thought she would snap
But the doc's fine elixir
Soon did fix her
And she went and had a mighty big crap . . .

There was much discussion about Jack
And the line of hair down his back
Despite all the rumour
Jack explained with humour
'All it does is point down to my crack . . .'

The big buzz word these days is 'stress'
It's something people love to confess
Just between me and you
And the psychologist, too
It just means you've got yourself into a mess . . .

There's this girl with a runny nose
Just like a tap, it turns on and flows
She finds the right fix
A good dollop of Vicks
From 50 metres, she can now smell a rose.

I'm constantly, constantly reeling
From people asking 'How are you feeling?'
If I hear it once more
I'll jump off the floor
And bang my head on the ceiling.

There was once a gynaecological surgeon
Whose medical career began to burgeon
He was so smart
At the top of his art
He turned a prostitute back to a virgin.

Liars

There was a professional liar named Proctor
Who told everyone he was a doctor
He once told a nun
Her oven had a bun
A diagnosis that certainly shocked her.

A compulsive liar named Jones
Used to sell cheap mobile phones
But once he was gone
You couldn't turn it on
The ones he was selling were clones . . .

Hot Love

A boy from Melbourne named Arthur
Married his childhood sweetheart, Martha
But things got hazy
She went a bit crazy
Now he drills for oil in Karratha . . .

The well-endowed Ibrahim Azziz
Went to a fortune teller in Cadiz
She said, 'Life will be great.
You'll love and create.'
But it fell off, and life was a fizz . . .

There once was a girl named Muriel
Whose technique in bed was mercurial
She'd jump in the cot
And be so hot to trot
That after it, you need an epidur(i)al . . .

The world's greatest lover McDuff
Thought he'd get never enough
Then he met Slow-hand Sadie
The Marathon Lady
Poor McDuff, he ran out of puff . . .

There once was a girl named Roxanne
Who knew how to get her man
She would look quite demure
Throw out the lure
And then store him away in a can . . .
A wild womaniser named Bert
Loved chasing a bit of skirt
But a girl named Hacker
Gave him the nutcracker
That was the end of Bert the flirt . . .

There once was a girl named Christina
My god, there was nobody leaner

Her hips and her waist
Were not to my taste
But when she stripped off, there was nobody keener.

A boastful young man named McDuff
Met what he thought was a little bit of fluff
But the talented Rosa
Recognized he was a poser
And soon left McDuff in a huff.

What a strange guy was Oedipus Rex
Very confused about sex
He went to this shrink,
Who said 'I think
You better make your mother your ex . . .'

One little mouse ran across the floor
And met his girlfriend behind the door
They ran to the clover
Where nature took over
And before you knew it there were four . . .

The car hoons love to screech a tyre
In front of the schoolgirls they admire
They spin the wheels
Amid admiring squeals
And leave a trail of smoke and fire.

FAMILY LIMERICKS

D espite the determination of many people to equate the limerick purely with sex, it still survives as an ingenious, enjoyable method of providing commentary, making political/social points, or just being odd and whimsical.

Here is a selection of limericks from across the years to the very present, by both acknowledged writers and that most prolific of authors, 'Anonymous', that can be read and enjoyed by people of all ages.

Animals

There was a young fellow called Mark
Who would swim out to sea in the dark
On these night-time trips
He saw lots of ships
Until he was ate by a shark.

There were three little birds in a wood
Who always sang hymns when they could
What the words were about
They could never make out
But they felt it was doing them good.

An elephant born in Tibet
One day in its cage wouldn't get.
So its keeper stood near
Stuck a hose in its ear
And invented the first Jumbo jet.

There was an old man of Boolong
Who frightened the birds with his song
It wasn't the words
Which astonished the birds
But the horrible dooble ontong.

There was a young man who was bitten
By twenty-two cats and a kitten
Cried he, 'It is clear
My end is quite near
No matter! I'll die like a Briton!'

A hungry old goat called Heather
Was tied up with an old bit of leather.
In a minute or two
She has chewed it right through
And that was the end of her tether.
                    – Celia McMaster

There was an old lady of Harrow
Whose views were exceedingly narrow
At the end of her paths
She built two bird baths
For the different sexes of sparrow.

There was an old maiden from Fife
Who had never been kissed in her life
Along came a cat
And she said, 'I'll kiss that.'
But the cat answered, 'Not on your life.'

There was a young man of Bengal
Who went to a fancy-dress ball
He went, just for fun
Dressed up as a bun
And a dog ate him up in the hall.

Said a fervent young lady of Hammels
'I object to humanity's trammels
I want to be free!
Like a bird! Like a bee!
Oh, why am I classed with the mammals!'
                    – Morris Bishop

An eccentric old person of Slough
Who took all his meals with a cow
Always said, 'It's uncanny
She's so like Aunt Fanny.'
But he never would indicate how.

There once was a dancing black bear
Who instead of a hat wore a pair
Of boots on his head
'It's the two step,' he said
'And feels like I'm walking on air.'

– J. Patrick West

Disasters

A daring young lady of Guam
Observed, 'The Pacific's so calm
I'll swim out for a lark'
She met a large shark
Let us now sing the Nineteenth Psalm.

There was an old man who averred
He had learned how to fly like a bird.
Cheered by thousands of people
He leapt from the steeple
This tomb states the date it occurred.

There was a queer lady named Harris
Whom nothing could ever embarrass
Till the bath salts she shook
In the bath that she took
Turned out to be Plaster of Paris!

A bottle of perfume that Willie sent
Was highly displeasing to Millicent
Her thanks were so cold
That they quarrelled, I'm told
Through that silly scent Willie sent Millicent.

A sensitive girl named O'Neill
Once went up in the big ferris wheel
But when half-way around
She looked down at the ground
And it cost her a two-dollar meal.

A new servant maid named Mariah
Had trouble in lighting the fire
The wood being green
She used gasoline
Her position by now is much higher!

A housewife called out with a frown
When surprised by some callers from town
'In a minute or less
'I'll slip on a dress.'
But she slipped on the stairs and came down.

There was a young man from the city
Who saw what he thought was a kitty
To make sure of that
He gave it a pat
They buried his clothes, what a pity!

I sat next to the Duchess at tea
Distressed as a person could be
Her rumblings abdominal
Were simply phenomenal
And everyone thought it was me!

Rebecca, a silly young wench
Went out on the Thames to catch tench
When the boat was upset
She exclaimed, I regret
A five-letter – and in French!

The village was giddy with rumours
Of a goat that was suffering tumours
Cans and library paste
Were quite to his taste
But he choked on Elizabeth's bloomers.

A railroad official at Crewe
Met an engine one day that he knew
Though he nodded and bowed
The engine was proud
And cut him – it cut him in two.

There was a young fellow named Hyde
Who fell through an outhouse and died
His unfortunate brother
Fell through another
And now they're in-turd side by side.

Said a foolish householder of Wales
'An odour of coal-gas prevails.'
She then struck a light
And later that night
Was collected in seventeen pails.

There was a daft gardener from Leeds
Who swallowed six packets of seeds
In a month the poor ass
Was all covered in grass
And he could not sit down for the weeds.

There was a young fellow named Weir
Who hadn't an atom of fear
He indulged in a desire
To touch a live wire
Most any last line will do here . . .

There was a young man of South Bay
Making fireworks one summer day
He dropped his cigar
In the gunpowder jar
There was a young man of South Bay . . .

There was an old man of Tarentum
Who gnashed his false teeth till he bent 'em
When they asked him the cost
Of what he had lost
He replied: 'I can't say, I just rent 'em.'

'I must leave here,' said Lady De Vere
'For those damp airs don't suit me, I fear.'
Said her friend, 'Goodness me!
If they do not agree
With your system, why eat pears, my dear?'

There was a young fellow from Tyne
Put his head on the South-Eastern Line
But he died of ennui
For the 5:53
Didn't come till a quarter past nine.

An unfortunate dumb mute from Kew
Was trying out sings that were new
He did them so fast
That his fingers at last
Got tangled and fractured a few.

A collegiate damsel named Breeze
Weighed down by BAs and Lit. D's
Collapsed from the strain
Alas, it was plain
She was killing herself by degrees . . .

There was a young lady of Florence
Who for kissing professed a great abhorrence
But when she'd been kissed
And found what she'd missed
She cried till the tears came in torrents.

There was a young lady of York
Who was shortly expecting the stork
When the doctor walked in
With a businesslike grin
A pickaxe, a spade and a fork.

There was an old lady of Rye
Who was baked by mistake in a pie
To the household's disgust
She emerged through the crust
And exclaimed with a yawn, 'Where am I?'

There was a young lady of Lynn
Who was so uncommonly thin
That when she essayed
To drink lemonade
She slipped through the straw and fell in.

There was a young man from Crew
Who wanted to build a canoe
He went to the river
And found with a shiver
He hadn't used waterproof glue.

                              Lorna Bain

Abbreviations

This is a clever way of using shortened names and references:
She frowned and called him Mr.
Because, in sport, he kr.
And so in spite
That very night
This Mr. kr. sr.

In this limerick, the word 'number' is abbreviated to 'No.'
When you think of the hosts with No.
Who are slain by the deadly cuco.,
It's quite a mistake
Of such food to partake
It results in a permanent slo.

*Once you run with Rt. as 'Right' and Rev. as 'Reverend',
you are in business:*
The sermon our Pastor Rt. Rev.
Began, may have had a rt. clev.,
But his talk, though consistent
Kept the end so far distant
That we left, since we felt he mt. nev.

*Here, 'oz.' stands for the old-fashioned weight of an
'ounce':*
A girl who weight many an oz.
Used language I dare not pronoz.
For a fellow unkind
Pulled her chair out behind
Just to see, so he said, if she'd boz.

Clothes

There was a young lady of Wilts
Who walked to the Highland on stilts
When they said 'Oh, how shocking,
To show so much stocking.'
She answered, 'Well, what about kilts?'

When she bought some pyjamas in Cheltenham
A lady was asked how she felt in 'em
She said, 'Winter's all right
But on a hot night
I'm afraid that I'm going to melt in 'em.

There once was a lady named Erskine
Who had remarkable fair skin
When I said to her Mabel
'You'd look well in sable.'
She answered, 'I'm best in my bearskin.'

A thrifty young fellow from Shoreham
Made brown paper trousers and wore 'em
He looked nice and neat
Till he bent in the street
To pick up a pin then he tore 'em.

There was a young lady named Choate
Whose pleasure it was to emote
She would say with a tear
'I am not wanted here!'
Then get up and take off her coat.
                        – William J Smith

Employment

A canner, exceedingly canny
One morning remarked to his granny,
'A canner can can
Anything that he can
But a canner can't can a can, can he?'
                        – Carolyn Wells

Fishy Tales

There was a young fellow named Fisher
Who was fishing for fish in a fissure
When a cod with a grin
Pulled the fisherman in
Now they're fishing the fissure for Fisher.

An oyster from Kalamazoo
Confessed he was feeling quite blue
'For,' he said, 'as a rule
When the weather turns cool
I invariably get in a stew!'

Food & Drink

There was an old lady of Brooking
Who had a great genius for cooking
She could bake sixty pies
All the same size
And tell which was which without looking.

There was an old man of Calcutta
Who spoke with a terrible stutter
At breakfast he said,
'Give me b-b-b-bread,
And b-b-b-b-b-b-b-butter.'

Teetotallers Larry and Mary
Said, 'Fresh milk makes us strong, so be wary.'
In the yard about three
They shouted with glee,
'Come join us, we're looting a dairy.'

A clever old gourmet named Sam
Used tubers for sweetening lamb.
He at times, lacking those,
Substituted his toes,
Declaring: 'I yam what I am.'

There once was a schoolboy named Hannibal
Who won local fame as a cannibal
By eating his mother
His father and brother
And his two sisters, Gertrude and Annabelle.

A cannibal bold of Penzance
Ate an uncle and two of his aunts
A cow and her calf
An ox and a half
And now he can't button his pants.

There was an old man of Peru
Who dreamt he was eating his shoe
He woke in the night
In a terrible fright
And found it was perfectly true . . .

To his wife said a grumbler named Dutton
'I'm a gourmet, I am, not a glutton.
For ham, jam, or lamb,
I don't give a damn
C'mon, let's return to our mutton.'

There was a young lady from Ickenham
Who went on a bus trip to Twickenham
She drank too much beer
Which made her feel queer
So she took off her boots and was sick-in-'em . . .

There was an old lady of Ryde
Who ate some green apples and died
The apples fermented
Within the lamented
Making cider inside 'er inside . . .

An amazing fast runner called Murray
Was always in a great hurry
The reason they say
Was the trip to Bombay
Where he sampled a Vindaloo curry . . .
                    – Andrew Henderson

I sat next to the duchess at tea
It was just as I feared it would be
Her rumblings abdominal
Were simply phenomenal
And everyone thought it was me . . . !

A braunschweiger eater named Kurst,
Thought that his stomach would burst.
But his doctor said,
'Nay! Your stomach's okay;
I'd say that your liver is wurst ...'

There once was a lady named Lynn
Who was so uncommonly thin,
That when she assayed
To drink lemonade,
She slipped through the straw and fell in!

There once was a hermit named Green
Who grew so abnormally lean
And flat, and compressed
That his back touched his chest
And sideways he couldn't be seen.

Foolish Behaviour

There was a strange creature named Marks
Whose idea of diversions and larks
Was stirring up tramps
Disturbing boys' camps
And defacing nude statues in parks.

There was an old lady of Herm
Who tied bows on the tail of a worm
Said she, 'You look festive
But don't become restive
You'll wriggle 'em off if you squirm.'

There was a young lady of Tottenham
Her manners, she'd wholly forgotten 'em
While at tea at the Vicar's
She took off her nickers
Explaining she felt much too hot in 'em.

There was a young girl from Asturias
Whose temper was frantic and furious
She used to throw eggs
At her grandmother's legs
A habit unpleasant but curious.

There was an old codger of Broome
Who kept a baboon in his room
'It reminds me,' he said,
'Of a friend who is dead.'
But he never would tell us of whom.

Said the peeping tom of Fort Lee
'Peeping ain't what it's cracked up to be
I lose all my sleep
And I peep and I peep
And I find them all peeping at me.'
                              – Morris Bishop

High Society

Miss Vera De Peyster Depew
Disdained anything that was new
She said 'I do not
Know exactly What's What
But I know, without question, Who's Who . . .'

Curious Logic

There was a young lady of Crete
Who was so exceedingly neat
When she got out of bed
She stood on her head
To make sure of not soiling her feet.

There was a faithhealer of Deal
Who said 'Although pain isn't real
If I sit on a pin
And it punctures my skin
I dislike what I fancy I feel.'

As they fished his old plane from the sea
The inventor just chortled with glee
'I shall build,' and he laughed
'A submarine craft
And perhaps it will fly. We shall see.'

A young schizophrenic named Struther
When told of the death of his mother
Said, 'Yes, it's too bad
But I can't feel too sad
After all, I still have each other . . .'

There once was a pious young priest
Who lived almost wholly on yeast
'For,' he said, 'it is plain
We must all rise again
And I want to get started at least.'

Said Oedipus Rex, growing red
'Those head-shrinkers, would they were dead!
They make such a pother
Because I love mother
Well, should I love father instead?!'

There was an old lady who said
When she found a thief under her bed,
'Get up from the floor,
You're too near the door
And you may catch a cold in your head.'

There was a young lady named Rood
Who was such an absolute prude
That she pulled down the blind
When changing her mind
Lest a curious eye should intrude.

There was a fat lady of Clyde
Whose shoelaces once came untied
She feared that to bend
Would display her rear end
So she cried and she cried and she cried.

There was a young woman named Eily
Who valued candle ends highly
When no one was looking
She used them for cooking
'It's wicked to waste,' she said dryly.

An important young man from Quebec
Had to welcome the Duchess of Teck
So he bought for a dollar
A very high collar
To save himself washing his neck.

There was an old widower named Doyle
Who wrapped his wife up in tin foil
He thought it would please her
To stay in the freezer
And anyway outside she'd spoil.

There was a fat man from Lahore
The same shape behind as before
They did not know where
To offer a chair
So he had to sit down on the floor.

There was an odd fellow of Tyre
Who constantly sat on the fire
When asked, 'Are you hot?'
He said, 'Certainly not.
I'm James Winterbotham, Esquire.'

An amoeba named Sam and his brother
Were having a drink with each other
In the midst of their quaffing
They split their sides laughing
And each of them now is a mother.

A rocket explorer named Wright
Once travelled much faster than light
He set out one day
In a relative way
And returned on the previous night.

*And this involves a scientific rule applying to the theory
of relativity:*
A fencing instructor named Fisk
In duels was terribly brisk
So fast was his action
The Fitzgerald contraction
Foreshortened his foil to the disk.

Maths

There was an old man who said 'Do
Tell me how I'm to add two and two
I'm not very sure
That it doesn't make four
But I fear that is almost too few.'

A Turk named Abdullah Ben Barum
Has sixty-five wives in his harem
When his favourite horse died
'Mighty Allah,' he cried,
'Take a few of my wives, I can spare 'em.'

Monsters

There once was a plesiosaurus
Who lived when the world was all porous.
But fainted with shame
When it first heard its name
And departed long ages before us.

Said the monster deep down in Loch Ness
'How I long for a change of address
Without this pollution
And constant confusion
From the tourists who make such a mess!'

There once was a phantom called Pete
Who never would play, drink or eat.
He said, 'I don't care
For a coke or éclair –
Can't you see that I'm dead on my feet.'

There once was a pale apparition
Who suffered from grave malnutrition
Said mum, 'You'll be a ghost
If you don't eat your toast.'
Answered he, 'That's just superstition.'

– Ann McGovern

A sea serpent saw a big tanker
Bit a hole in her side and then sank her.
It swallowed the crew
In a minute or two
And then picked its teeth with the anchor.

A werewolf named Wendy is fair
So long as the sun is up there
But when the moon rises
She puts on disguises
With fangs and a lot of coarse hair . . .

– Ann McGovern

A ghoul and his girl for a lark
Went strolling one night in the park
They stopped under a light
And the ghoul cried in fright
'Eek! Quick dear, get back in the dark.'

Music

A tutor who tooted the flute
Tried to tutor two tooters to toot.
Said the two to the tutor
'Is it harder to toot, or
To tutor two tooters to toot?'
                   – Carolyn Wells

A tone-deaf person from Tring
When somebody asked him to sing
Replied, 'It is odd
But I cannot tell 'God
Save the Weasel' from 'Pop Goes the King'.

An opera star named Maria
Always tried to sing higher and higher
Till she hit a high note
Which got stuck in her throat
And she entered the heavenly choir.

There was a young girl in the choir
Whose voice rose higher and higher
Till one Sunday night
It rose quite out of sight
And they found it next day on the spire.

Playing with Words

Here was a young lady from Woosester
Who ussessed to crow like a roosester
She ussessed to climb
Seven trees at a time
But her sister ussessed to boosester.

There was a young girl in the choir
Whose voice rose hoir and hoir
Till it reached such a height
It was clear out of seight
And they found it next day in the spoir.

There once was a bonnie Scotch laddie
Who said as he put on his plaidie
'I've just had a dish
O' unco' guid fish.'
What had he had? Had he had haddie?

There was a good Canon of Durham
Who fished with a hook and a worrum
Said the dean to the Bishop
'I've brought a big fish up
But I fear we will have to inter'm.'

A rare old bird is the pelican
His beak holds more than his belican
He can take in his beak
Enough food for a week
I'm damned if I know how the helican!

There was a young lady of Twickenham
Whose boots were too tight to walk quickenham
She wore them in style
But after a while
She pulled them both off and was sickenham

An unpopular youth of Cologne
With a pain in his stomach did mogne
He heaved a great sigh
And said 'I would digh
But the loss would be only my ogne.'

An old couple living in Gloucester
Had a beautiful girl but they loucester
She fell from a yacht
And never the spacht
Could be found where the cold waves had toucester.

A boy who played tunes on a comb
Had become such a nuisance at homb
His ma spanked him, and then –
'Will you do it again?'
And he cheerfully answered her, 'Nomb.'

There was a young lady of Munich
Whose appetite simply was unich.
She contentedly cooed
'There's nothing like food,'
As she let out a tuck in her tunich.

The principal food of the Siouxs
Is Indian maize, which they briouxs
And then failing that
They'll eat any old hat
A glove, or a pair of old shiouxs.

There once was a choleric colonel
Whose oaths were obscene and infolonel
And the chaplain, aghast
Gave up protest at last
But wrote them all down in his jolonel.

A fellow who lived in New Guinea
Was known as silly young nuinea
He utterly lacked
Good judgment and tacked
For he a told a plump girl she was skuinea.

Some day 'ere she grows too antique
My girl's hand in marriage I'll sicque
If she's not a coquette
Which I'd greatly regruette
She shall share my ten dollars a wicque.

A bright little maid in St Thomas
Discovered a suit of pajhomas
Said the maiden, 'Well, well!
Whose they are I can't tell
But I'm sure those garments St Mhomas.'

There were two young ladies of Birmingham
I know a sad story concerningham
They stuck needles and pins
In the right reverend shins
Of the Bishop engaged in confirmingham.

A globetrotting man from St Paul
Made a trip to Japan in the faul
One thing he found out
As he rambled about
Was that Japanese ladies St Taul.

Think about American beer brewers:
There was a young girl named Anheuser
Who said that no man could surprise her
But old Overholt
Gave her virtue a jolt
And now she is sadder Budweiser . . .

A lady there was of Antigua
Who remarked to her spouse, 'What a pigua!'
He retorted, 'My queen
Is it manners you mean
Or do you refer to my figua?'

There's a notable family named Stein
There's Gertrude, there's Ep and there's Ein
Gert's prose is in the bunk
Ep's sculpture is junk
And no-one can understand Ein.

A barber who lived in Batavia
Was known for his fearless behavia
An enormous baboon
Broke into his saloon
But he murmured, 'I'm damned if I'll shavia.'

A lady, an expert on skis
Went out with a man who said 'Plis'
'On the next precipice
Will you give me a kice?'
She said, 'Quick! Before somebody sis!'

Said a lively young nurse out in Padua
To her master, 'Please, sir, you're a dadua
I've come for some pins
For to wrap up the twins
And to hear you remark, sir, how gladua.'

There was a young poet of Trinity
Who, although he could trill like a linnet, he
Could never complete
Any poem with feet
Saying 'Idiots,
Can't you see
That what I'm writing
  happens
   to be
  Free
Verse?'

A very polite man named Hawarden
Went out to plant flowers in his gawarden
If he trod on a slug
A worm or a bug
He would instantly say, 'I begpawarden.'

                         – Carolyn Wells

There was an old maid of Genoa
I blush when I think what Iowa
She's gone to her rest
And it's all for the best
Otherwise, I would borrow Samoa . . .

A cheese that was aged and grey
Was walking and talking one day
Said the cheese, 'Kindly note
My mama was a goat
And I'm made out of curds, by the whey . . .'

A fly and a flea in a flue
Were imprisoned, so what could they do?
Said the fly, 'Let us flee!'
'Let us fly!' said the flea.
So they flew through a flaw in the flue.

There was a young man named Hall
Who fell in the spring in the fall
'Twould have been a sad thing
Had he died in the spring.
But he didn't – he died in the fall.

Take the curious case of Tom Pettigrew
And Hetty his sister. When Hetty grew
As tall as a tree
She came just to Tom's knee
And did Tom keep on growing. You bettigrew.

                         – David Mc Cord

Politics

A Labor MP was so raucous
He caused uproar in the Caucus
'If we don't get it right
On election night
The Tories will forever stalk us . . .'

People

Said a fervent young lady of Hammels
'I object to humanity's trammels
I want to be free!
Like a bird! Like a bee!
Oh, why am I classed with the mammals!'

                         – Morris Bishop

The poor benighted Hindu
He does the best he can do
He sticks to caste
From first to last
For pants he makes his skin do.

A pious old Jew from Salonika
Said, 'For Christmas, I'd like a harmonica.'
His wife, to annoy him,
Said, 'Feh! That's for goyim!'
And gave him a Jew's harp for Chanukah.

Religious

There was a young curate of Minster
Who admonished a giddy young spinster
For she used, on the ice
Words not at all nice
When he, at a turn, slid ag'inst her.

We thought him an absolute lamb
But when he sat down on the jam
On taking his seat
At our Sunday School treat
We all heard the Vicar say '- - - -!
er – stand up, please, while I say grace.'

There was a kind curate of Kew
Who kept a large cat in a pew
There he taught it each week
A new letter of Greek
But it never got further than Mu.

There was a young parson named Perkins
Exceedingly fond of small gherkins
One summer at tea
He ate forty-three
Which pickled his internal workin's.

An indolent vicar of Bray
His roses allowed to decay
His wife more alert
Bought a powerful squirt
And said to her spouse, 'Let us spray.'

                     – Langford Reed

Revenge

His mother-in-law's leather lung
Got her young son-in-law so unstrung
That her pushed her unseen
In a chopping machine
And canned her and labelled her 'Tongue.'

Romance

Said the fair-haired Rebecca of Klondike
'Of you, I'm exceedingly fond, Ike
To prove I adore you
I'll dye, darling for you
And be a brunette, not a blonde, Ike.'

There was a dear lady of Eden
Who on apples was quite fond of feedin'
She gave one to Adam
Who said, 'Thank you, Madam.'
And then both skedaddled from Eden.

*A little French phrase in this one, referring, of course, to a
bottle of liquid fun.*
There was an old maid of Vancouver
Who captured a man by manoeuvre
She jumped on his knee
With some rare eau de vie
And nothing on earth could remove her.

Said a pretty young student named Smith,
Whose virtue was largely a myth
'Try as hard as I can
I can't find a man
Who it's fun to be virtuous with.'

She frowned and called him Mister
Because in sport he kissed her
And so, in spite
That very night
This mister kissed her sister.

You have written a sonnet, said Chloe
On my bosom so rounded and snowy
You have sent me some verse on
Each part of my person
That's lovely. Now do something, Joey!

A cautious young girl from Penzance
Decided to take just one chance
She wavered, then lo,
She let herself go
Now all of her sisters are aunts.

A sculptor remarked, 'I'm afraid
I've fallen in love with my trade
I'm much too elated
With what I've created
And, chiefly, the woman I've made.'

The classical sculptor called Phidias
Whose knowledge of art was insidious
Once carved Aphrodite
Without any nightie
Which shocked all the purely fastidious.

A young country boy from Pitlochery
Kissed a much made-up girl in a rockery
When he tasted the paint
He cried, 'Lassie, this ain't
A real kiss at all, it's a mockery.'

There was a fierce soldier from Parma
Who lovingly fondled his charmer
Said the maiden demure
'It's delightful, I'm sure
But it'd be better without all that armour.'

A stripteaser up in Fall river
Caused a sensitive fellow to quiver
The aesthetic vibration
Brought soulful elation
Besides, it was good for his liver.

There was a young charmer named Sheba
Whose pet was a darling amoeba
This queer blob of jelly
Would lie on her belly
And blissfully murmur, 'Ich liebe.'

Here, it helps to know that Bicester is pronounced 'Bister.'
When her daughter got married in Bicester
Her mother remarked as she kissed her
'That fellow you've won
Is sure to be fun
Since tea, he's kissed me and your sister.'

There was a young poet of Thusis
Who took twilight walks with the Muses
But these nymphs of the air
Are not quite what they were
And the practice has led to abuses.

A young girl from old Abeystwyth
Brought grain to the mill to get grist with
But the millers' son Jack
Sighed, 'A lass and a lack,'
And united the things that they kissed with.

'Austerity now is the fashion,'
Remarked a young lady with passion
Then she glanced at the bed
And quietly said
'But there's one thing no-one can ration.'

As Mozart composed a sonata
The maid bent to fasten her garter
Without delay
He started to play
Un poco piu apassionata.

There was a young maiden of Siam
Who said to her love, young Kiam
'If you kiss me, of course
'You will have to use force
'But God knows you are stronger than I am.'

There was a young person named May
Who never let men have their way
But a brawny young spark
One night in the dark . . .
Now she goes to the park every day.

There was a young writer named Smith
Whose virtue was largely a myth
We knew that he did it
He couldn't have hid it
The question was only who with.

A much-worried mother once said
'My dear, you've been kissing young Fred
Since six; it's now ten
Do it just once again
And then think of going to bed.'

A girl who would not be disgraced
Would flee from all lovers in haste
It all went quite well
Till one day she fell
She sometimes still dreams that she's chaste.

A free-living damsel named Hall
Once went to a birthcontrol ball
She took an appliance
To make love with science
But nobody asked her at all.

There once was a lady from Nantes
Tres chic and tres elegante
But her mouth was so small
It was no use at all
Except for la plume de ma tante.

There was a young girl from Detroit
Who at kissing was very adroit
She could pucker her lips
Into total eclipse
Or open them out like a quoit.

When the civil engineer took advantage
Of a lovely young lady of Wantage
The County Surveyor
Said 'You'll have to pay her
For you've altered the line of her frontage.'

A corpulent maiden named Kroll
Had an idea exceedingly droll
At a masquerade ball
Dressed in nothing at all
She twisted the rock and the roll.

It is time to make love. Douse the glim
The fireflies flicker and dim.
The stars lean together
Like birds of a feather
And the loin lies down with the limb.

                              – Conrad Aiken

There was a young lady from Kent
Who said that she knew what it meant
When men asked her to dine
Upon lobster and wine
She knew. Oh, she knew! But she went.

There once was a lady named Mabel
So ready, so willing, so able
And so full of spice
She could name her own price
Now Mabel's all wrapped up in sable.

There was an old monk in Siberia
Whose existence grew gradually drearier
Till he broke from his cell
With a hell of a yell
And eloped with the Mother Superior.

On Matilda's white bosom there leaned
The cheek of a low-minded fiend
But she yanked up his head
And sarcastically said
'My boy. Won't you ever be weaned?'

There was a young lady named banker
Who slept while her ship lay at anchor
She awoke in dismay
When she heard the mate say
'Hi! Hoist up the top sheet and spank'er.'

There once was a lady with such graces
That her curves cried aloud for embraces
'You look,' cried he
'Like a million to me
Invested in all the right places.'

There was a young fellow named Tait
Who dined with his girl at 8.08
But I'd hate to relate
What that fellow named Tait
And his tete-a-tete ate at 8.08!

– Carolyn Wells

There were once two young people of taste
Who were beautiful down to the waist
So they limited love
To the regions above
And thus remained perfectly chaste.

There was a young man of high station
Who was found by a pious relation
Making love in a ditch
To – I won't say a bitch –
But a woman of no reputation!

There was an old fellow from Croydon
Whose cook was a cute little hoyden
She would sit on his knees
While shelling the peas
Or pleasanter duties employed on.

There was a young maid of Ostend
Who swore she'd hold out to the end
But, alas, halfway over
From Calais to Dover
She done what she didn't intend.

There was a young lady named Kate
Who necked in the dark with her date
When asked how she fared
She said she was scared
But otherwise doing first-rate.

There was a young lady of Eton
Whose figure had plenty of meat on
She said, 'Wed me, Jack
And you'll find that my back
Is a nice place to warm your cold feet on.'

A certain young chap named Bill Beebee
Was in love with a lady named Phoebe
'But,' said he, 'I must see
What the clerical fee
Be Before Phoebe be Phoebe B. Beebee.'

Two beauties who dwelt by the Bosphorous
Had eyes there were brighter than phosphorous
The sultan cried 'Troth!
I'll marry you both!'
But they laughed, 'I'm afraid you must toss for us.'

There is a young girl of Kilkenny
Who is worried by lovers so many
That the saucy young elf
Means to raffle herself
And the tickets are two for a penny.

There once was a maitre d'hotel
Who said, 'They can all go to hell!
They make love to my wife
And it ruins my life
For the worst is, they do it so well.'

There was a young man from Racine
Who invented a funny machine
Concave and convex
It suited either sex
The goddmanedest thing ever seen.

Three lovely young girls from St Thomas
Attended dance-halls in pyjamas
They were fondled all summer
By sax, bass and drummer
I'm surprised that by now they're not mamas.

There was a young wife who begat
Three husky boys, Nat, Pat and Tat.
They all yelled for food
And a problem ensued
When she found there was no tit for Tat.

There was a most finicky lass
Who always wore panties of brass
When asked, 'Don't they chafe?'
She said, 'Yes, but I'm safe
From pinches and pins in the grass.'

There was a young gaucho named Bruno
Who said, 'Love is all that I do know.
A tall girl is fine
A short one's divine
But a llama is numero uno.'

A cute debutante from St Paul
Wore a newspaper dress to a ball
The dress caught on fire
And burnt her entire
Front page, sporting section, and all.

There was a young student at Johns
Who attempted to fondle the swans
Whereupon said the porter
'Oh, pray take my daughter
The birds are reserved for the dons.'

There is a sad rumour that Mona
Goes around in a black net kimona
Don't think for a minute
There's anything in it
Anything much besides Mona.

To his bride said the lynx-eyed detective
'Can it be that my eyesight's defective?
Has your east tit the least but
The best bit of the west tit?
Or is it a trick of perspective?'

There is a young blue blood named Maud
A frightful society fraud
In company she
Is as cold as could be
But get she alone, oh my Gawd!

There once was a rake known as Baker
Who to seduce a fair Quaker
And when he had done it
She straightened her bonnet
And said, 'I give thanks to my maker.'

There was a pert lass from Madras
Who had a remarkable ass
Not rounded and pink
As you probably think
It was grey, had long ears, and ate grass.

There was a young lady named Hopper
Who came a society cropper
She determined to go
To Bordeaux with her beau ...
The rest of the story's improper.

There was a young lady from Thrace
Whose corsets would no longer lace.
Her mother said, 'Nelly,
There's more in your belly
Than ever went in through your face.'

A lissom psychotic named Jane
Once kissed every man on a train
Said she, 'Please don't panic
I'm just nymphomanic
It wouldn't be fun were I sane.'

A handsome young bastard named Ray
Was conceived on the Rue de la Paix.
According to law
He can name you his maw
But as for his pa, je ne sais . . .
                              – John F. Moore

Said a calendar model named Gloria
'So the men can enjoy real euphoria
You pose as you are
In Jan, Feb and Mar
Then in April they wanna see moria!'

Have you heard about Madame Lupescu
Who came to Romania's rescue?
It's a wonderful thing
To be under King
Is democracy better? I eskyou!

In the Garden of Eden sat Adam
Disporting himself with his madam.
She was filled with elation
For in all of creation
There was only one man, and she had'm.

A dentist named Archibald Moss
Fell in love with the dainty Miss Ross
Since he held in abhorrence
Her Christian name Florence
He renamed her his dear dental Floss.

A gardening nut from O'Hare
Grew apples and grapes in his hair
One day on the beach
He met a young peach
Now the peach and the nut are a pear.

A lady and expert on skis
Went out with a man who said, 'Please
On the next precipice
Will you give me a kiss?'
She said, 'Quick before somebody sees.'

School

A right-handed fellow named Wright
In writing 'write' always wrote 'right'
Where he meant to write 'right'
If he'd written 'write' right
Wright would not have wrought rot writing 'rite' . . .

Said a boy to his teacher one day
'Wright has not written 'rite' right, I say.'
And the teacher replied
As the error she eyed
'Right! Wright write 'write' right, right away . . . !'

Nantucket . . .

The word Nantucket appears in many, many limericks –
usually pointing to a very obvious ending! But the best
known doesn't go that way.

In fact, the original Nantucket five lines was written by
William Cosmo Monkhouse (read more about him in the
'How it all Began' chapter).

A newspaper reprinted this limerick in the 1920s and
sparked a series of follow-ups. This is how it progressed:

The Princeton Tiger ran the original Monkhouse limerick:
There once was a man from Nantucket,
Who kept all of his cash in a bucket,
But his daughter, named Nan,
Ran away with a man,
And as for the bucket, Nantucket.

It was followed up by this piece in the Chicago Tribune:
But he followed the pair to Pawtucket,
The man and the girl with the bucket;
And he said to the man,
He was welcome to Nan,
But as for the bucket, Pawtucket.

*It went on from there, with other papers and individuals
jumping into the fray, carrying the story forward:*
Then the pair followed Pa to Manhasset,
Where he still held the cash as an asset,
But Nan and the man
Stole the money and ran,
And as for the bucket, Manhasset.

– Exchange

Of this story we hear from Nantucket,
About the mysterious loss of a bucket,
We are sorry for Nan,
As well as the man,
The cash and the bucket, Pawtucket.

– Pawtucket Times

Nan's man had a plan to skedaddle,
And take off with the cash to Seattle,
On his arrival out west
The cash he'd invest,
Then kick back on a farm and raise cattle.
                    – Bob Watson, Lake Forest, CA

Then the man took the cash to Cotuit
Leaving Nan and her Pa home to rue it.
Pa said, 'Daughter most clearly,
I must beat him severely,
Said Nan in response, 'Please Gotuit!'

The thief was then followed to Hingham,
By the sheriff whose goal was to bringham
Back to suffer the stares
Of a jury of peers.
'If he's guilty by God we will Hingham!'

So the loot was returned to Nantucket.
It was jail for the man who had tucket.
But the judge was not rash,
Gave the lawyers the cash,
Leaving Nan and her Pa with the bucket.
– Thomas J. Annacone, Yorktown Heights, NY

Sport

There was a young lady of Venice
Who used hard-boiled eggs to play tennis
When they said: 'It seems wrong.'
She remarked: 'Go along!
You don't know how prolific my hen is.'

There was a young man of Belfast
Who ran in a race and came last
He said, 'That's enough!
I'm all out of puff.'
As a tortoise came thundering past.
  – Carol Stevenson

Teeth

There was an old man of black heath
Who sat on his set of false teeth
Said he with a start
'Oh Lord, bless my heart!
I've bitten myself underneath.'

The Body

This is a trio by poet Anthony Euwer
The Hands
The hands, they were made to assist
In supplying the features with grist
There are only a few
As a rule, about two
And are hitched to the end of the wrist.

The Face
As a beauty I'm not a great star
There are others more handsome by far
But my face, I don't mind it
Because I'm behind it
It's the folks in front that I jar!

The Smile
No matter how grouchy you're feeling
You'll find the smile more or less healing
It growths in a wreath
All around the front teeth
Thus preserving the face from congealing.

A classical scholar from Flint
Developed a curious squint
With her lefty-handed eye
She could scan the whole sky
While the other was reading small print.

An angry young husband named Bickett
Said, 'Turn yourself round and I'll kick it
You have painted my wife
In the nude to the life
Do you think, Mr. Greene, that was cricket?

The mouth of a glutton named Moto
Was the size that no organ should grow to
It could take in with ease
Six carrots, ten peas
And a whole baked potato in toto.

There was an old lady from Kent
Whose nose was remarkably bent
One day, they suppose
She followed her nose
For no-one knows which way she went.

A girl being treated for a hernia
Remark to her doctor, 'Goldernia,
When slicing my middle
Be sure not to fiddle
With matters that do not concernya.'
                    – John Galsworthy

An odd-looking girl from Devizes
Had eyes of two different sizes
The one was so small
It was nothing at all
But the other, it won several prizes.

There was an old skinflint named Green
Who grew so abnormally lean
And flat and compressed
That his back squeezed his chest
And sideways he couldn't be seen.

There was a young maid who said, 'Why
Can't I look in my ear with my eye?
If I give my mind to it
I'm sure I can do it.
You never can tell till you try.'

There was a young teacher named Phinn
Whose legs were incredibly thin
When he did the high kicks
They resembled drum sticks
And he played the Top 10 on his chin.
                              – Lesley Calder

A dancing-girl came from St Gall
With a mouth so exceedingly small
That she said, 'It would be
Much more easy for me
To do without eating at all!'

There was a young lady named Rose
Who had a huge wart on her nose
When she had it removed
Her appearance improved
But her glasses slipped down to her toes.

The Drink

There was a young fellow named Sydney
Who drank till he ruined his kidney
It shrivelled and shrank
As he sat there and drank
But he had a good time, didn't he?

There was a . . .

There was a young girl, a sweet lamb
Who smiled as she entered a tram
After she had embarked
The conductor remarked
'Your fare.' And she said, 'Yes, I am . . .'

There was a young man of Montrose
Who had pockets in none of his clothes
When asked by his lass
Where he carried his brass
He said, 'Darling, I pay through the nose.'

There once was a girl of New York
Whose body was lighter than cork
She had to be fed
For six weeks upon lead
Before she went out for a walk.

There was a young lady from Lynn
Who was sunk in Original Sin
When they said, 'Do be good,'
She replied, 'If I could . . .
But I'd do wrong right over ag'in.'

There once was a boy of Baghdad
And inquisitive sort of a lad
He said 'Let us see
If a sting has a bee.'
And very soon found out it had.

There was a brave damsel from Brighton
Whom nothing could possible frighten
She plunged in the sea
And with infinite glee
Rode away on the back of a Triton.

There was an old lady of Wales
Who lived upon oysters and snails
Upon growing a shell
She exclaimed, 'It is well
Now I'll never wear bonnets or veils.'

There's a tiresome young man in Bay Shore
When his fiancé cried, 'I adore
The beautiful sea!'
He replied, 'I agree
It's pretty, but what is it for?'

– Morris Bishop

From the age when lamps were gas-driven:
There was a young woman of Glasgow
Whose party proved quite a fiasco
At nine-thirty, about
The lights all went out
Through a lapse on the part of the Gas Co.

There was a young person from Perth
Who was born on the day of his birth
He was married, they say
On his wife's wedding day
And died when he quitted this earth.

There was once a spinster from Wheeling
Endowed with such delicate feeling
That she thought any chair
Should not have its legs bare
So she kept her eyes fixed on the ceiling.

There was a young lady of Lancashire
Who once went to work as a bank cashier
But she scarcely knew
$1 + 1 = 2$
So they had to revert to a man cashier.

There was a young man at the War Office
Whose brain was not good as a store office
Every warning severe
Simply went in one ear
And out at the opposite orifice.

There's a clever old miser who tries
Every method to e-con-omise
He said with a wink
'I save gallons of ink
By simply not dotting my i's.'

There was a young lady from Kent
Who always said just what she meant
People said, 'She's a dear
So unique, so sincere.'
But they shunned her by common consent.

There was a young girl from Gloucester
Whose parents thought they had lost her
From the fridge came a sound
And at last she was found
The trouble was how to defrost her.

There was an old fellow from Tyre
Who constantly sat on a fire
When asked, 'Are you hot?'
He said, 'Certainly not
I'm James Winterbottom, esquire.'

There was an old man of Darjeeling
Who travelled from London to Ealing
It said on the door
'Please don't spit on the floor.'
So he carefully spat on the ceiling.

There was a young woman named Dotty
Who said as she sat on the potty
'It isn't polite
To do this in sight
But then who am I to be snotty?'

There was a lady called Millicent
Who hated the perfume that Willie sent
So she sent it to Liz
Who declared, 'What a swiz
It's that silly scent Willie sent Millicent.'

There was an old man of Peru
Who dreamt he was eating a shoe
He awoke in the night
With a terrible fright
And found it was perfectly true!

There once was a lady named Gail,
Who decided to have a garage sale.
She sold all her wares,
Including the chairs.
Now she's one upstanding female.

There was once a young lady diver
Held her breath a long time for a fiver
And she doubled it when
She was offered a ten
But at twenty we had to revive her.

Travel

In Paris some visitors go
To see what no person should know
And then there are tourists
The purist of purists
Who say it is quite comme il faut.

There was a young lady from Crewe
Who wanted to catch the 2.02
Said a porter, 'Don't worry,
Or hurry, or scurry,
It's a minute or two to 2.02 ...'

There was a young lady named Bright
Who travelled much faster than light
She started one day
In the relative way
And returned on the previous night ...

There was a young lady from Spain
Who was dreadfully sick on the train
Not once – but again
And again and again
And again and again and again ...

Tricky Words

These limericks rely on the use of English names and places that are not pronounced as they appear. In some cases, it gives the opportunity for the writer to carry the spelling right through the verse. In the following limerick, for example, things are a bit clearer when you realise that Magdalen is pronounced 'maudlin'.

A beauty, a perfect divinity
Till twenty retained her virginity
The boy up at Magdalen
Must have been dawdlin'
It wouldn't have happened at Trinity.

In this limerick, Sydenham is pronounced 'sidden-hm'.
Said the man to his wife down in Sydenham
'My trousers, where have you hidden 'em
It's perfectly true
That they aren't brand new
But I foolishly left half a quid in 'em.'

Here, Drogheda rhymes with 'annoyed her'.
A young Irish servant in Drogheda
Had a mistress who often annogheda
Whereupon she would swear
In a language so rare
That thereafter nobody emplogheda.

Here, Beauchamp is pronounced 'beecham'.
Said a bad little youngster named Beauchamp
'Those jelly tarts, how shall I reauchamp?
To my parents I'd go
But they always so "No",
No matter how much I beauschamp.'
– Carolyn Wells

Let the mind wander with this one. 'Salisbury' used to be known as 'Sarum', and Hampshire is still often referred to as 'Hants'.
There was a young curate of Salisbury
Whose manners were halsibury-scalisbury
He would wander around Hampshire
Without any pampshire
Till the vicar compelled him to walisbury.

Here, Wemyss is pronounced 'weems':
There was a young lady named Wemyss
Who, it semyss was afflicted with dremyss
She would wake in the night
And, in terrible fright
Shake the bemyss of the house with her scremyss.

This is an American limerick, with Mich pronounced 'Mish'.
There's a girl out in Ann Arbor, Mich.,
To meet who I never could wich.,
She'd gobble ice-cream
Till with colic she'd scream
Then order another big dich.

And in this limerick, Cholmondeley is pronounced 'chumly'.

There was once a maiden named Cholmondeley
Who everyone said was quite colmondley
Yet the maid was so shy
That when strangers were by
She always would stand around dolmondeley.

Playing with Words

Two starry-eyed, reckless young beaux
Were held up and robbed of their cleaux.
While the weather is hot
They won't miss them a lot,
But what will they do when it sneaux?

When out on the warpath the Siouxs,
March single file never by tiouxs,
And by 'blazing' the trees,
Can return at their ease,
And their way through the forest ne'er liouxs.

There was a young man from the Bronx
Who, when offered a piece, said, 'No thonx.'
He said, 'I declare,
I prefer solitaire,
And all that I do is just yonx.'

Whoops . . .

Evangeline Alice du Bois
Committed a dreadful faux pas
She loosened a stay
In her decollete
Exposing her je ne sais quoi.

Writing Limericks

There was a young man of Japan
Who wrote verse that would never scan
When they said, 'But the thing
Doesn't go with a swing,'
He replied, 'Yes, but I always like to get as many words into
the last line as I possibly can!'

There once was a man from the sticks
who liked to write limericks.
But he failed at the sport
Because he wrote them too short . . .

There once was a man from Peru,
Whose limericks always end on line two . . .

The limerick is furtive and mean.
You must keep her in close quarantine.
Or she sneaks to the slums
And promptly becomes
Disorderly, drunk and obscene!

When you've done quite the best that you can
But your limerick still doesn't scan
And the lines won't run true
And the whole thing's askew
Don't worry about it, just write whatever comes
   into your head.

A poet named Heinrich Himmerlich
Finally published a limerick
His maniacal chortle
Proclaimed: 'I'm immortal!'
But alas, his renown was ephemerid.

There was an old man
From Peru, whose lim'ricks all
Looked like haiku. He
Said with a laugh 'I
Cut them in half, the pay is
Much better for two.'

A limericker woke from his snooze
Got into his best running shoes
And worked up a sweat
With a butterfly net
As he tried to recapture the muse.

Our lesson tonight
Considers the plight
Of the dyslexic poet named Chad
Who writes limericks abysmally bad
He can't get it right.

Answering Machine Message

There once was a man from Nantucket
Who was old, but not yet kicked the bucket
Don't be a creep,
At the sound of the beep,
Leave a message or you can just f . . . orget about anyone
   calling you back!

New Technology

There once was a hacker named Ken
Who inherited truckloads of Yen
So he built him some chicks
Of silicon chips
And hasn't been heard from since then.

There was a rash fellow called Weir
Who hadn't an atom of fear
He indulged a desire
To touch a live wire
And it blew him from there to here.

When I die, I just hope my main squeeze
Stores my body in very deep freeze.
Then when I thaw out,
My nurses will shout,
And it will astound all the MD's.

A girl on a southern plantation
Was the product of insemination.
So each Fathers' Day
She would send a bouquet
To a syringe in a far away nation.

Oh, so Vain

There was a bus driver named Peter,
Who could not have looked any neater.
But his moustache looked funny,
When he combed it with honey,
Thus making his kisses much sweeter.

A pet store employee named Blair
Was missing a small patch of hair.
A tarantula crawled
To the spot that was bald
And nobody noticed it there!

Places

There was a farmer from Leeds
Who ate six packets of seeds
It soon came to pass
He was covered with grass
And he couldn't sit down for the weeds!

An epicure dining at Crewe
Found a very large bug in his stew.
Said the waiter, 'Don't shout
And wave it about,
Or the rest will be wanting one too.'

There once was a man in Bombay
Who was making explosives one day.
He dropped his cigar
In the gunpowder jar
There once WAS a man from Bombay.

There was a Young Lady of Portugal
Whose ideas were excessively nautical
She climbed up a tree
To examine the sea
But the Admiral cried 'Come down you naughty gal!'

There was a young woman from Bright
Whose speed was much faster than light.
She set out one day
In a relative way,
And returned on the previous night.

There was an Old Man of the Isles
Whose face was pervaded with smiles:
He sang 'High Dum Diddle',
And played on the fiddle,
Balancing eels on his nose all the whiles.

There was an Old Man of Columbia,
Who was thirsty demanded some beer;
But they brought it quite hot,
In a small copper pot,
A hot beer is not much good cheer.

There once was a lady from Brazil
Who climbed up a very big hill
When she fell down
She rolled into town
And felt like a bit of a dill.

If you go to Tibet, where you think
You'll discover that old Missing Link
Do beware; don't forget he
Might well be a Yeti
With furry big feet that may stink.

SEX AND THE BAWDY LIMERICK

From a comic scenario in the 1820s, the limerick soon evolved into a social parody, a political manifest, and a comment on the heroes, villains and events of the times. Then along came sex ...

Whether we like it or not, the limerick has become the sniggering vehicle for amazing tales about men and women with grossly enlarged genitalia, bizarre sexual practices and an insatiable appetite for all things crass. Big boobs, giant penises and awe-inspiring sexual conquests abound. Bestiality, incest and sodomy regularly appear, along with jibes at the clergy and racial taunts.

Literary lovers of the limerick lament this shift, particularly to the point nowadays where many people incorrectly assume that a limerick must always be about sex. Of course, it's easy to conclude that this is a trend that developed over the last few decades, since the 1960s overthrew many conservative values and changed society's views on sex and relationships. But that is not so! Far from it, as the following pages reveal.

The sexual theme started as far back as the late 19th century and took off from there. You might be surprised to see limericks from Queen Victoria's times being so blunt and outrageous in their style.

Among the groupings in this chapter, we have assembled a range of limericks in their time-frames across three major periods – the late 19th century, 1900 to 1930 and 1930 to 1960. In their own way, they show how society – and its approach to sex – evolved.

It's interesting to note, too, the explosion of limericks with blatant sexual overtones that appeared after World War 2. It seems that the cessation of hostilities and the arrival of peace suddenly freed up the spirit and let loose a torrent of feelings and thoughts that had been suppressed and repressed during the bleak times of the war.

Like it or not, a history of the limerick would not be valid if it didn't contain limericks about sex – after all, they are the most quoted ones. Usually, if you hear a limerick these days it is about sex.

But we warn the faint-hearted to approach this chapter with some degree of trepidation. Some of the limericks contain imagery that is beyond belief, and we have had to use a couple of words that are not usually used around the dining table, although we have gone for the '****' version to ease the impact.

So, here we go. Almost everything you wanted – or didn't want! – to know about sex, limerick style.

Comic

There was a young maid from Madras
Who had a magnificent ass;
Not rounded and pink,
As you probably think
It was grey, had long ears, and ate grass . . .

The drugs that we use when we're ailing
Go by different names for retailing
Tylenol's acetamenophen.
Advil's Ibuprofen.
And Viagra is Mycoxafailing . . .

A proper young person Mal Grissing
Announced he had given up kissing.
'I strike out at once
For something that counts,
And besides my girl's front teeth are missing.'

There was an old sculptor named Phidias
Whose knowledge of art was invidious.
He carved Aphrodite
Without any nightie
Which startled the purely fastidious.

There was an old man named Peach,
Who mislaid his pearly false teeth.
Laid 'em down in a chair,
Plumb forgot they were there,
Then sat down and got bit from beneath!

Withdrawal, according to Freud,
Is a very good thing to avoid.
If practised each day
Your balls would decay
To the size of a small adenoid.

Under the spreading chestnut tree
The village smith he sat,
Amusing himself
By abusing himself
And catching the load in his hat.

There was a young man of Madras
Who was having a roll in the grass.
Then a cobra-capello
Said, 'Hello, young fellow!'
And bit a piece out of his ass.

Winter is here with his grouch,
The time when you sneeze and slouch.
You can't take your women
Canoein' or swimmin',
But a lot can be done on a couch.

A young girl who was no good at tennis,
But at swimming was really a menace,
Took pains to explain,
'It depends how you train,
I was once a street-walker in Venice.'

As the elevator car left our floor,
Big Sue caught her tits in the door;
She yelled a good deal,
But had they been real,
She'd have yelled considerably more.

A crooner who lived in Lahore
Got his balls caught in a door.
Now his mezzo soprano
Is rather piano
Though he was a loud basso before.

The Cork Screw in Two Parts

There was a young girl from New York
Who plugged up her twat with a cork.
A woodpecker or two
Made the grade, it is true,
But it totally baffled the stork

Till along came a man who presented
A tool that was strangely indented.
With a dizzying twirl
He punctured that girl
And thus was the corkscrew invented.

Ecclesiastical

So grimly the Abbot said, 'Look,
Wanking's a sin in my book,
Inadvertent or not.
Tie your dick in a knot
Or start sleeping with Annie the cook.'

A gentle old lady I knew
Was dozing one day in her pew;
When the preacher yelled 'Sin!'
She said, 'Count me in!
As soon as the service is through!'

We thought we were going to die
When the minister raised his arms high
The benediction to say,
But it wasn't his day,
He'd forgotten to zip up his fly!

There once was a boring young Reverend
Who preached till it seemed he would never end.
His hearers, en masse,
Got a pain in the ass,
And prayed for relief of their nether end.

There was a young Rabbi from Peru
Who was vainly attempting to screw
His wife said 'Oi, vey
If you keep up this way
The Messiah will come before you do.'

A nudist by name Roger Peet,
Loved to dance in the snow and the sleet,
But one chilly December
He froze every member,
And retired to a monkish retreat.

There was a young fellow named Sistall,
Who shot three old maids with a pistol.
When 'twas known what he'd done,
He was given a gun
By the unmarried curates of Bristol.

There was a young lady of Tottenham
Whose manners - well, she had forgotten 'em
While at tea at the vicar's
She took off her knickers
Explaining she felt much too hot in 'em.

There was a straight parson named Billings
Who talked about God and such things.
But his secret desire
Was to join a mixed choir
With nice ladies with whom he'd have flings.

The bishop of Winchester Junction
Found his phallus would no longer function.
So in black crepe he wound it,
Tied a lily around it,
And solemnly gave it last unction.

I once had the wife of a Dean
Seven times while the Dean was out skiin'.
She remarked with some gaiety,
'Not bad for the laity,
But the bishop once managed thirteen.'

There was a young lady from Kew
Who said, as the curate withdrew:
'I prefer the dear vicar;
He's longer and thicker;
Besides, he comes quicker than you.'

From the depths of the crypt at St Giles
Came a scream that could be heard for miles.
Said the vicar, 'Goodness Gracious,
It's Father Ignatius,
He's forgotten the Bishop has piles.'

There was a young girl from Odessa,
A rather unblushing transgressor.
When sent to the priest
The lewd little beast
Began to undress her confessor.

There's a man in the Bible portrayed
As one deeply engrossed in his trade.
He became quite elated
Over things he created,
Especially the women he made.

When Paul the Apostle lay prostrate,
And leisurely prodded his prostate,
With pride parabolic
His most apostolic
Appendage became an apostate.

A progressive professor named Tinners
Held classes each evening for sinners.
They were graded and spaced
So the very debased
Would not be held back by beginners.

Pets

Said a rather promiscuous duck,
'With the drakes I just don't get no luck;
They approach me all slick
But then paddle off quick
They can't seem to muster the pluck.'

The bustard's a fortuitous fowl,
Who has but small reason to growl.
He avoids illegitimacy
By the simple expediency
Of the use of an alternate vowel.

There was a bulldog named Caesar,
Saw a cat and decided to tease 'er,
But she scratched and she spit,
Till the big bulldog quit,
Now Caesar just sees 'er and flees 'er!

There was a young mouse named Gracian.
As a lifeguard he was a sensation.
All the lady mice raved,
And screamed to be saved,
By his mouse-to-mouse resuscitation!

Two elephants, Harry and Faye,
Couldn't kiss with their trunks in the way,
So they boarded a plane,
They're now kissing in Maine,
'Cause their trunks got sent on to L.A.

A rooster became quite dismayed,
With an orange in a nest displayed.
He called to his chicks,
'Mom's up to her tricks!
Look at the orange "marma-laid".'

There was an old maid in Peru
Who'd a dog and a cat and a gnu.
From a sailor named Harrot
She bought an old parrot,
And he threw in a young cockatoo.

There was a young man named McFee
Who was stung in the balls by a bee.
He made oodles of money
By oozing pure honey
Every time he attempted to pee.

There was a young hunter named Shepherd
Who was eaten for lunch by a leopard.
Said the leopard, 'Egad!
You'd be tastier, lad
If you had been salted and peppered!'

A mouse in her room woke Miss O'Dowd
Who was frightened and screamed very loud
Then a happy thought hit her
To scare off the critter
She sat up in bed and just meowed.

There was a young curate of Kew
Who kept a tom cat in a pew
He taught it to speak
Alphabetical Greek,
But it never got further than Mu.

An amorous bull known as Morton
Was arrested for stampin' and snortin'.
When released from his cell
He was madder'n hell
For the season had passed for cavortin'.

There was a fat turkey named Sam
Who gobbled whenever he ran.
He came out of the bush
Presenting his tush
And was shot up the arse by a man.

There was an old lady who cried
She felt sad and desolate inside
She sold her fat cat
That sat on a mat
But it fell in a pot and got fried.

The sultan got sore at his harem
And thought up this plan for to scare 'em:
He caught a wee mouse
Which he loosed in the house
The confusion is called harem-scarem.

A serious thought for today,
Is one that may cause you dismay.
Just what are the forces
That bring little horses
If all of the mares say, 'Nay!'

There once was a king rat
Who said this and later said that
He zigged one day
And went the wrong way
He should have zagged, so that was that.

A wonderful fish is the flea,
He bores and he bites on me.
I would love, indeed,
To watch him feed,
But he bites me where I cannot see.

One evening a workman named Rawls
Fell asleep in his old overalls.
And when he woke up he
Discovered a puppy
Had bitten off both of his balls.

Two roosters were bragging away,
Of their talent for waking the day.
As they stood there aghast,
Dawn sneaked quietly past,
And was announced by a donkey's loud bray.

When a devious fellow named Fleagle
Proceeded to marry his beagle
He replied to the preacher
'Yes, I do take this creature.'
While the dog said: 'You're sure this is legal?'

Observations

'It's true,' confessed Jane, Lady Torres,
'That often I beg lifts in lorries.
When the men stop to piss
I see things that I miss
When I travel alone in my Morris.'

A surly and pessimist Druid,
A defeatist, if only he knew it,
Said, 'The world's on the skids,
And I think having kids
Is a waste of good seminal fluid.'

Woe, alack, and alas!
I'm held together by intestinal gas!
Each time I fart,
Something falls apart.
See! There's a crack in my ass!

Van Gogh found a whore who would lay,
And accept a small painting as pay.
'Vive l'Art!' cried Van Gogh,
'But it's too f**cking slow,
I wish I could paint ten a day!'

There once was a young man named Lanny
The size of whose prick was uncanny.
His wife, the poor dear,
Took it into her ear,
And it came out the hole in her fanny.

There once was a woman named Nor,
Whose chest was as flat as the floor.
It is sad to be said
That in dark, in the bed,
Men sucked on her shoulder blades more.

When the judge, with his wife having sport,
Proved suddenly two inches short,
The good woman declined,
And the judge had her fined
By proving contempt of the court.

When a corpulent spinster named Snow
Was approached by a dwarf for a blow,
She replied, 'I have pride!
Your request is denied!
I could never, sir, stoop quite that low.'

There was a young girl of Darjeeling
Who could dance with such exquisite feeling
There was never a sound
For miles around
Save of fly-buttons hitting the ceiling.

As a kid when we rode on the bus
Deep questions we'd often discuss:
'Would it come off divine,
Or just blow out her spine,
If Superman did it with Lois?'

An unfortunate groom was Walter
Left standing alone at the altar
The source of the rift
His prenuptial gift
A bridle and bit and a halter . . .

As the strings played a soft obligato
The soprano's shrill notes were staccato
As she crouched on the face
Of the powerful bass
And enjoyed his tremendous vibrato.

A little adultery spices
Our lives, but just look at those prices!
If they charge all that dough,
Men can't buy it, you know,
And there'll be a frustrational crisis.

There once was a girl from Decatur
Got laid by a big alligator.
But, we never knew
The result of that screw,
'Cause after he laid her, he ate her.

There was an odd fellow named Lars,
Who'd pick up young ladies in bars.
He'd scarce get to know them,
Then hoist up and throw them,
And that's how he'd grant them the stars.

An amoeba named Sam, and his brother,
Were having a drink with each other.
In the midst of their quaffing,
They split themselves laughing
And each of them now is a mother.

Poorer, but wiser is she,
It cost her a trip 'cross the sea.
But, she learned with great joy,
Unlike an American Boy,
Scots don't have to unzip to pee.

A pretty young lady named Vogel
Once sat herself down on a molehill.
A curious mole
Nosed into her hole
Ms Vogel's OK, but the mole's ill.

She's called 'The Professional Sinner'
Twenty bucks and she lets you get in her.
If given a fifty,
Things really get nifty.
Ten more and she'll take you to dinner.

A young corporate banker named Beatty
Once had an affair with a lady.
It wouldn't have been
Such a sin, had she been
A couple of years under eighty.

Mr Jones was a bass in the choir,
Yet a man who loved playing with fire
He wrestled a bear
Who didn't play fair
Now he's singing a full octave higher.

A wizard, the moment he smelled her
Fell in love with the witch Esmerelder
And, obsessed with the notion
Tried to copy her potion
But his formula failed and repelled her.

Hot Love

There was a young man of high station
Who was found by a pious relation
Making love in a ditch
To, I won't say a bitch,
But a woman of no reputation.

There was a young lady called Wylde
Who kept herself quite undefiled
By thinking of Jesus,
Contagious diseases,
And the bother of having a child.

There was a young lady of Louth
Who suddenly grew very stout.
Her mother said, 'Nelly,
There's more in your belly
Than ever went in through your mouth.'

There was a young fellow from Dallas
Who enjoyed doing things with his phallus.
So many tricks did he try
It became, by and by,
Little more than a leather-tough callous.

In the soap opera heard in Gomorrah,
The heroine wakes up in horror
To find that a prick
Nearly three inches thick
Is halfway up her tune-in-tomorrow.

There was a fat lady of China
Who'd a really enormous vagina,
And when she was dead
They painted it red,
And used it for docking a liner.

There once was a priest from Gibraltar
Who wrote dirty jokes in his Psalter.
An inhibited nun
Who had read everyone
Made a vow to be laid on his altar.

A milkmaid there was, with a stutter,
Who was lonely and wanted a futter.
She had nowhere to turn,
So she diddled a churn,
And managed to come with the butter.

There was a young lady of Trent
Who said that she knew what it meant
When he asked her to dine,
Private room, lots of wine,
She knew, oh she knew! But she went!

There was a young girl from Hong Kong
Whose cervical cap was a gong.
She said with a yell,
As a shot rang the bell,
'I'll give you a ding for a dong!'

There was a young lady from Munich
Who was had in a park by a eunuch.
In a moment of passion
He shot her a ration
From a squirt-gun concealed 'neath his tunic.

The Book of God's beneath you,
The Man of God's above you.
Salvation pole
Is in your hole
Now wiggle your ass to save your soul.

Nymphomaniacal Alice
Used a dynamite stick for a phallus.
They found her vagina
In North Carolina,
And her asshole in Buckingham Palace.

A rooster residing in Spain
Used to diddle his hens in the rain.
'I give them a bloody
Good time when it's muddy:
Which keeps them from getting too vain.'

There was a young girl of Rangoon
Who was blocked by the Man in the Moon.
'Well, it has been great fun,'
She remarked when he'd done,
'But I'm sorry you came quite so soon.'

There was a young person of Tottenham
Whose manners, Good Lord!, she'd forgotten 'em.
When she went to the vicar's,
She took off her knickers,
Because she said she was hot in 'em.

A beautiful lady named Psyche
Is loved by a fellow named Ikey.
One thing about Ike
The lady can't like
Is his prick, which is dreadfully spikey.

There was a young lady whose joys
Were achieved with incomparable poise.
She could have an orgasm
With never a spasm
She could fart without making a noise.

There was a young girl of Detroit
Who at f***ing was very adroit:
She could squeeze her vagina
To a pinpoint, or finer,
Or open it out like a quoit.

A certain young man of St Paul
Consistently practised withdrawal.
This quaint predilection
Created such friction,
He soon had no foreskin at all.

There was a young man of Devizes
Whose balls were of different sizes.
His tool, when at ease,
Hung down to his knees,
Oh, what it must be when it rises!

There was a young lady named Hall
Wore a newspaper dress to a ball.
The dress caught on fire
And burned her entire
Front page, sporting section, and all.

There was a young girl of Penzance
Who boarded a bus in a trance.
The passengers f***ed her,
Likewise the conductor.
The driver shot off in his pants.

There was a young girl whose frigidity
Approached cataleptic rigidity,
Till you gave her a drink,
When she quickly would sink
In a state of complaisant liquidity.

The nipples of Sarah Sarong,
When excited, were twelve inches long.
This embarrassed her lover
Who was pained to discover
She expected no less of his dong.

There was a young man of Madras
Who was f***ing a girl in the grass,
But the tropical sun
Spoiled half of his fun
By singeing the hair off his ass.

There was a young lady of Dexter
Whose husband exceedingly vexed her,
For whenever they'd start
He'd unfailingly fart
With a blast that damn nearly unsexed her.

There was a young lady named Flo
Whose lover had pulled out too slow.
So they tried it all night
Till he got it just right . . .
Well, practice makes pregnant, you know.

I know of a fortunate Hindu
Who is sought in the towns that he's been to
By the ladies he knows,
Who are thrilled to the toes
By the tricks he can make his foreskin do.

There was a young fellow named Bryce
Who remarked 'They say bigamy's nice;
But just two's a bore,
I prefer three or four,
For the plural of spouse it is spice.'

The Good Ship Venus

The good ship's name was *Venus*,
Her mast a towering penis,
Her figurehead
A whore in bed
A pretty sight, by Jesus!

The first mate's name was Andy,
By God, he was a dandy,
They broke his cock
With chunks of rock
For conking in the brandy.

The second mate was Morgan,
By God, he was a Gorgon,
Nine times a day
Fine tunes he'd play
On his reproductive organ.

Then in search of new sensation
In the forms of recreation,
The ship was sunk
In a wave of gunk
From mutual masturbation.

* * *

Bragging

Each man that Miss Jones chose to wed with,
She first liked to paint the town red with,
For having made merry,
She then became very
Aroused and fantastic in bed with.

Said my wife as she stood on a rostrum,
'I don't mind if I don't have colostrum,
But I'll take an option
If your child's for adoption
Though I cannot bear kids, I can foster 'em.'

It's a helluva fix that we're in
With the geographical spread of sin
Which causes juvenile delinquency
With increasing frequency
By the Army, the Navy, and Errol Flynn.

There once was a guy on a ski,
Who desperately needed to pee.
He loosened his clothes,
His penis soon froze,
As an icicle down to his knee.

A licentious old justice of Salem
Used to catch all the harlots and jail 'em.
But instead of a fine
He would stand them in line,
With his common-law tool to impale 'em.

There was a young man, Mussolini,
Who found he had seven bambini.
He said, 'If I thought
That the griddle was hot,
I'd never have put in the weenie!'

A handsome young widow named Vi
Seduced all the wardens nearby.
When the sirens said, 'Woo!'
What else could they do
To extinguish the gleam in her eye?

There was a young man from Maine
Whose prick was as strong as a cane;
It was almost as long,
So he strolled with his dong
Extended in sunshine and rain.

There's a lot has been said 'bout the breast
Like how nicely they feel when they're pressed.
But when push comes to shove,
In this business of love,
It's 'what's' 'tween the legs that is best.

There once was a man named Crockett
He stuck his cock in a socket.
Some son-of-a-bitch
Turned on the switch
And Crockett went up like a rocket.

There once was a freshman named Lin,
Whose tool was as thin as a pin.
A virgin named Joan,
From a Bible-belt home,
Said, 'This won't be much of a sin.'

Celebrations

A nudist from over the Pass,
Thinks the Fourth of July is a gas,
His cock and balls, too
He paints red, white, and blue,
And sticks a flag pole up his ass.

Easter Sunday a young boy, Stan Snead,
Popped a stiff one as long as a reed.
And did he turn beet red,
When Pastor Fred loudly said,
'He is risen. He is risen indeed!'

Employment

A publisher once went to France
In search of a tale of romance;
A Parisian lady
Told a story so shady
That the publisher made an advance.

There once was a tailor named Fred,
Who always got knots in his thread.
Said the frustrated tailor,
'I should be a sailor . . .
The knots they tie get them ahead.'

A prodigious soprano named Dotty
Ate a dinner of beans and biscotti
Then, I'm sad to impart,
Her intestines took part
In her duet with poor Pavarotti.

A maiden at college, Miss Breeze,
Weighed down by B.A.'s and Lit. D's,
Collapsed from the strain,
Said her doctor, 'It's plain
You are killing yourself by degrees!'

When Picasso was tender in years
He considered some other careers
While reading reportage
Of imminent shortage
Of models with eyes in their ears.

A stubborn old butcher named Burke,
Who became quite annoyed by a clerk
And her constant reminders
'Don't sit on meat grinders,'
Got a little behind in his work.

Said a printer pretending to wit:
'There are certain bad words we omit.
It would sully our art
To print the word f - - -,
And we never, oh never, say sh - -!'

A cautious young chemist named Mound
Was surprised, but not hurt, when he found
That A mixed with B
In the presence of C
Made a hole (ringed with dirt) in the ground.

There once was a geologist named Wassail,
Who one day found a colossal fossil.
He could tell by the bend,
And the knob at the end,
That it was the peter of Paul, the apostle.

A confused driving student one night
Made a left by mistake at the light
Then she turned left twice more
With intent to be sure
For she knew that three wrongs make a right.

There was a chicken farmer from Hay,
Who found his hens wouldn't lay;
The trouble was Brewster,
His champion rooster;
You see, Brewster the rooster was gay!

Tom Duane, an elderly jockey,
Hung up his spurs and felt cocky.
'I've got saddle galls
On both of my balls.'
But the doctor wrote down, 'Gonococci.'

To the builder, the younger King Tut
The loan institutions were shut
'To build pyramids
Takes quids upon quids
And those rocks are a pain in the butt.'

We were painting the church steeple grey,
When the wind blew our brushes away.
We said to the pastor,
'What a disaster!'
He calmly replied, 'Let us spray.'

Johnny's new warehouse job was a bore.
Packing boxes all day was a chore.
For that job he had yearned
But it's one he'd have spurned
If the 'ware' hadn't sounded like 'whore'.

At the circus, a reporter named Peeks
Was impressed by the fat lady's cheeks
And announced his intentions
To describe her dimensions
Though he thought it might take him three weeks.

A taxi cab whore out at Ivor
Did the round trip for a fiver
Quite reasonable too
For a sightsee and screw
With a fifty cent tip to the driver.

A miner who bored in Brazil
Found some very strange rust on his drill.
He thought it a joke
Till the bloody thing broke
Now his tailings are practically nil.

A mortician who practiced in Fife
Made love to the corpse of his wife.
'How could I know, Judge?
She was cold, did not budge
Just the same as she'd acted in life.'

To his bride said the keen-eyed detective,
'Can it be that my eyesight's defective?
Has your east tit the least bit
The best of your west tit,
Or is it the faulty perspective?'

A young architect named Yorick
Who could, when feeling euphoric
Display for selection
Three kinds of erection,
Corinthian, Ionic and Doric!

There was a young tenor named Springer,
Got his testicles caught in a wringer.
He hollered in pain
As they rolled down the drain,
'There goes my career as a singer!'

There was a young lady named Hilda
Who went for a walk with a builder.
He knew that he could,
And he should, and he would
And he did, and he bloody near killed her!

A young entomologist, Bunny
Did something that I found quite funny.
She pulled down her pants
And went hunting for ants
By coating herself with fresh honey.

A bobby of Nottingham Junction
Whose organ had long ceased to function
Deceived his good wife
For the rest of her life
With the aid of a constable's truncheon.

There is a professor named Martin
From whom I'm about to be partin',
And on my way out,
He may hear me shout,
'It's your face I'd sure like to fart in.'

There once was a midwife of Gaul
Who had hardly no business at all.
She cried, 'Hell and damnation!
There's no procreation,
God made the French penis too small.'

A mathematician named Hall
Has a hexahedronical ball
And the cube of its weight
Times his pecker's, plus eight
Is his phone number, give him a call.

We once had a clerk named Pyle
Who had an affair with our file.
'Twas strewn askew
From K through to Q,
And the P's were all sticky and vile.

There was a young farmer named Fritz
Who planted an acre of tits.
They came up in the fall,
Pink nipples and all,
And he chewed them all up into bits.

There was an old sculptor named Phidias
Whose knowledge of art was invidious.
He carved Aphrodite
Without any nightie
Which startled the purely fastidious.

The guys in uniform were not cops
They were thieves, the robbers of shops
The cops were at a meeting
The mayor they were greeting
Cos' the mayor thought the cops were the tops!

There once was an old man of Esser,
Whose knowledge grew lesser and lesser,
It at last grew so small
He knew nothing at all,
And now he's a college professor.

There once was a tattooist named Clarke
Whose urge to render was stark.
He put roses on hogs
And bare-shaven dogs
And nudes on drunks in the park.

A quick witted astronaut, Dwight,
When asked 'bout his upcoming flight,
Did he have worry one
'Bout landing on the sun?
'Heck no, we're landing at night!'

A geneticist living in Delft
Scientifically played with himself,
And when he was done
He labelled it 'Son',
And filed it away on the shelf.

There once was a poet named Dan,
Whose poetry never would scan.
When told this was so
He said, 'Yes, I know
It's because I try to put every possible syllable into the
    very last line that I can!'

A seamstress at Epping-on-Tyne
Used to peddle her tail down the line.
She first got a crown,
But her prices went down,
Now she'll fit you for ten pence or nine.

A poetess luscious and trim
Indulged in a rather strange whim
When composing a sonnet
She wore but a bonnet
And stripped herself bare for a hymn.

The life of a clerk of the session
Was strangled in psychic repression.
But his maladies ceased
When his penis increased
In straight geometric progression.

There once was a sailor from Wales,
An expert at pissing in gales.
He could piss in a jar
From the top-gallant spar
Without even wetting the sails.

There was an announcer named Herschel
Whose habits became controversial
Because when out wooing
Whatever he was doing
At ten he'd insert his commercial.

There once was a man from afar
Who bought a flamenco guitar;
When he painted it pink
It made others think
That his English was way below par!

There was a young plumber from Lee
Who was plumbing a maid by the sea
Said the maid, 'Stop your plumbing,
I hear someone coming!'
Said the plumber, still plumbing, 'It's me!'

There once was a handsome young actor;
While filming, he fell off a tractor.
Though not in his script,
He went to Egypt,
To visit the Cairo-practor.

A nymphomaniacal nurse
With a curse that was worse than perverse
Stuck a rotary drill
Up herself, for a thrill
And they carted her off in a hearse.

There was a young golfer named Lear
Who went to jail for a year
For an act quite obscene,
On the very first green,
Under a sign saying 'Enter course here.'

A maestro directing in Rome
Had a quaint way of driving it home.
Whoever he climbed
Had to keep her tail timed
To the beat of his old metronome.

A detective named Ellery Queen
Has olfactory powers so keen,
He can tell in a flash
By the scent of a gash
Who its previous tenant has been.

A neuropath-virgin named Flynn
Shouted before she gave in:
'It isn't the deed,
Or the fear of the seed,
But that big worm that's shedding its skin!'

An organist playing in York
Had a prick that could hold a small fork,
And between obbligatos
He'd munch at tomatoes,
To keep up his strength while at work.

There once lived a youth in Duluth,
Who aspired to a life as a sleuth.
But he soon changed his mind,
For it shocked him to find,
That the truth is so often uncouth.

A musician in gay Montebello
Amused herself playing the cello,
But not a solo,
For she used as a bow
The dong of a sturdy young fellow.

A dulcet-voiced callgirl named Shedd,
Who's cultured, well-spoken, well-bred,
Had achieved some renown
For her tone going down
There's a nice civil tongue in her head.

Though on takeoffs a pilot named Irving
Delighted in swooping and swerving
Going faster than sound
While still on the ground
His passengers found it unnerving.

Rose and the Hose

Four Verses

There was a young lady named Rose
Who'd occasionally straddle a hose,
And parade about squirting
And spouting and spurting,
Pretending she pissed like her beaux.

She was seen by her cousin named Anne,
Who improved the original plan.
She said, 'My dear Rose,
In this lowly old hose
Are all the best parts of a man.'

So, avoiding the crude and sadistic,
She frigged in a manner artistic:
At the height of her pleasure
She turned up the pressure,
And cried, 'Ain't it grand and realistic!'

They soon told the Duchess of Fyfe,
And her crony, the alderman's wife;
And they found it so pleasing,
And tickling and teasing
That they washed men right out of their life.

Food & Drink

There is a young girl from Poughkeepsie,
Known through the town as a gypsy.
If she has not a drink,
She gives ne'er a wink,
But, man, she puts out when she's tipsy.

There once was a lady named Perkins
Who loved to eat green gherkins
They thought them so nice
She ate too much spice
And pickled her internal workings.

On the chest of a barmaid at Yale
Was tattooed the price of each ale
Whilst on her behind
For the sake of the blind
Was precisely the same, but in Braille.

There was a young lady from Glynn
Who thought that to kiss was a sin.
But when she was tight,
It seemed quite all right,
So the gentlemen plied her with gin.

There was a young fellow named Matt,
When at the pub he likes to chat
'More precious than rubies
Are young girls with big boobies,
Or at least it is something like that.'

Writing Limericks

The ancient orthographer, Chisholm.
Caused a lexicographical schism
When he asked to know whether
'T were known which was better
To use 'g' or 'j' to spell 'jism'.

I remember consulting a Buddhist
About limericks that he thought the lewdest.
He replied as he leered,
'I like them quite weird:
They must deal with a fully dressed nudist.'

The limerick form is complex,
Its contents run chiefly to sex.
It burgeons with virgins
And masculine urgings
And swarms with erotic effex.

What a limerick is in a crunch
Is a bit like a loony's light lunch,
Though it briefly delights
It's just four nutty bites
Swallowed down with a ludicrous punch.

A limerick's a poetic antic
With undertones that are semantic.
It's best if it's rude,
Or crude, or just lewd,
And its meter is frequently frantic.

The limerick packs laughs anatomical
Into space that is quite economical.
But the good ones I've seen
So seldom are clean
And the clean ones so seldom are comical.

There was a young lady whose bonnet
Came untied when the birds sat upon it
But she said, 'I don't care!
All the birds of the air
Make my limerick seem like a sonnet.'

Thus endeth my lim'ricks, part two.
What next, you may ask, will I do?
Perhaps something bawdy,
Obscene, or just nawdy.
Who knows? If I don't, how can you?

Making Impressions

An old-fashioned person named Brett
Said, 'This sonnet my love will me get.'
Not having email
He sent it by snail.
Neither letter nor Brett have come yet.

A handsome young fellow called Campbell
Went out with some girls on a ramble.
They were pleased and impressed
By his sexy prowess,
But he cried, 'This is just the preamble!'

There was a homemaker named Pat,
Who couldn't sew, knit or tat.
She baked bread for the fair,
Won a blue ribbon there,
And said, 'Thank you, I kneaded that!'

A mason, one of the Malones
Put a coat of cement on his stones.
'They keep warmer at night,
And are bound to hang tight,
And not bruise themselves on my kneebones.'

There's a man in New York name of Bobby
Whose delight in himself was his hobby.
He rode the lift down,
While 'a goin' to town'.
He arrived when he came at the lobby

There was a young woman named Dottie
Who said as she sat on the potty,
'It isn't polite
To do this in sight,
But then, who am I to be snotty?'

A geologist named Dr Robb
Was perturbed by his thingamabob,
So he took up his pick
And whanged off his wick,
And calmly went on with his job.

There was a small girl called Louise
Whose backside was stung by some bees.
She rushed home to Mother
Who proceeded to smother
Her bottom with tubs of cream cheese.

A shapely young lady named Jenna
Coloured her pubic hairs with henna.
On a beach she was crude
Sunbathed in the nude.
She was promptly invited to dinnah . . .

From the whore whom they called Geraldine:
'When I think of the pricks that I've seen,
And all of the nuts
And the assholes and butts,
And the bastards like you in between . . .'

An efficient young fellow named Dave
Said, 'Think of the time that I save
By avoiding vacations
And sexy relations,
And taking a crap when I shave.'

There was a young fellow named Skinner
Who took a young lady to dinner.
At a quarter to nine
They sat down to dine;
At twenty to ten it was in her.

There was a young fellow named Tupper
Who took a young lady to supper.
At a quarter to nine
They sat down to dine,
And at twenty to ten it was up her.

Full ninety years old was friend Wynn
When he went to a hook shop to sin.
But try as he would,
It did him no good,
For all he had left was the skin.

There was a young fellow named Goody
Who claimed that he wouldn't, but would he?
If he found himself nude
With a gal in the mood,
The question's not would he, but could he?

There was a young lady named Gay,
Who was asked to make love in the hay.
She jumped at the chance
And took off her pants,
She was tickled to try it that way!

There's an over-sexed lady named Whyte
Who insists on a dozen a night.
A fellow named Cheddar
Had the brashness to wed her
His chance of survival is slight.

A young bodybuilder named Rex
Bought two bras to support his huge pecs
Wore the 48B
When he let them hang free,
And a black one with D-cups to flex.

'Last night,' said a lassie named Ruth,
'In a long-distance telephone booth,
I enjoyed the perfection
Of an ideal connection,
I was screwed, if you must know the truth.'

There was a young fellow named Perkin
Who was always jerkin' his gherkin.
His wife said, 'Now, Perkin,
Stop jerkin' your gherkin,
Because you're shirkin' your ferkin'.'

The cock of a fellow named Randall
Shot sparks like a big Roman candle.
He was much in demand,
For the colours were grand,
But the girls found him too hot to handle.

There was a little girl named Anna
Who asked her mother for a piano
Her mother said 'No'
And gave her a poh
She said, 'Now you can have your pee, Anna ...'

There was a young man named Hughes
Who swore off all kinds of booze.
He said, 'When I'm muddled
My senses get fuddled,
And I pass up too many screws.'

There was a fellow named Dave
Who just didn't know how to behave.
Until he met Mandy,
Who was ever so randy,
And now he's become her sex slave.

A wonderful tribe are the Sweenies,
Renowned for the length of their weenies.
The hair on their balls
Sweep the floor of their halls,
But they don't look at women, the meanies.

There was a young pessimist, Grotten,
Who wished he had ne'er been begotten,
Nor would he have been
But the rubber was thin,
And right at the tip it was rotten.

There was a young athlete named Grimmon
Who developed a new way of swimmin'
By a marvellous trick
He would skull with his prick,
Which attracted loud cheers from the women.

Crossed Wires . . .

An old maid phoned the desk and said, 'Joe,
What's the noise from that room down below?'
'Oh, they're holding,' he sighed,
'An Elk's Ball just inside.'
'Well then, tell them,' she said, 'to let go!'

Said an oak, 'It isn't nice to crow
But trees are so much purer, though;
The birds and the bees
Is all nasty sleaze:
Mighty oaks from little acorns grow.'

Lil married a rich old geezer
But the old dude just couldn't please her.
So she slipped him Viagra,
Then he flowed like Niagara,
And screwed 'til he died from the seizure.

In an earthquake, the best thing to do
Is to set about having a screw:
When you're done, you can say
In a nonchalant way,
'May I ask, did the earth move for you?'

Out of love for my newlywed Claire,
I decided to gift her an heir,
But she cried in disdain,
As my work proved in vain,
And the present got caught in her hair.

A randy young fellow named Payne
Wooed a lovely girl, but in vain,
For she swore when he kissed her,
So he slept with her sister
Again and again and again.

A lisping young man from Fort Worth,
With a dick of fantastical girth,
Once said with a grin,
As he coaxed it all in,
'I can thee that I'm not quite your firtht!'

A pitiful case is young Rex,
With his bulgingly masculine pecs,
And biceps the size
Of a weightlifter's thighs,
For he's thinking of changing his sex.

Amidst the confusion of a crowd,
Dirty Joe fondled young Miss Dowd.
She was shocked and afrighted,
And yet so excited,
That she moaned for help . . . but not too loud!

Two fussy old queers from Algiers
Were flustered and almost in tears,
For the buggers had spent
What they needed for rent,
And their landlord had said, 'No arrears.'

A man with venereal fear
Had intercourse in his wife's ear.
She said, 'I don't mind,
Except that I find
When the telephone rings, I don't hear.'

An old man who lived by the Nile
Had dysfunction that was erectile.
They grafted a boner
From an equine donor.
Now all the girls give him a smile.

A modest young girl named Oola
Once donned a grass skirt to dance Hula.
A cow ate the grass,
Exposing her ass,
Now she's no longer modest but coola.

A modern cinegraphic emporium
Is not just a super-sensorium
When the mood is terrific
It's an ultra-specific
Mutual masterbatorium.

A sculptor named Auguste Rodin
Did a sculpture once of a man.
He called him 'The Thinker,'
I call him 'The Stinker'
You can see he sits right on the can.

A werewolf whose name was Malone
Liked to dig up then gnaw on a bone.
'His tastes were lupine,
And now he's supine'
Are the words carved into his headstone.

There was a young man from St Paul's
Who read *Harper's Bazaar* and *McCall's*
Till he grew such a passion
For feminine fashion
That he knitted a snood for his balls.

There was a young lady from Chisworth
Who asked a young man, 'What is this worth?',
As she lifted her skirt,
He became quite alert
And declared, 'All I possess on this earth!'

There once was a puppy named Grover
Who lived in a city called Dover.
His master was odd,
And fed him green cod,
Then flattened him with his Land Rover.

There was an old man from China
Who wasn't a very good climber.
He slipped on a brick
Which severed his prick
And now he has a vagina.

There was a young lady named Kinter,
Who married a man in the winter.
The man's name was Wood,
And now, as they should,
The Woods have a cute little splinter . . .

There was a young girl of Spitzbergen
Where people all thought her a virgin,
Till they found her in bed,
With her quim very red,
And the head of a kid just emergin'.

To care for those stricken with gout
To soothe the fear and the doubt
'Twas her ambition, she
Always wanted to be
A nurse, but it didn't pan out.

To be brief, the great action was done
There was artfully planted a son
Through a bodkin that filled her,
And wonderfully thrilled her
More fun than a son of a gun.

A simple young farmer of Bray
Met a lass in his hayfield one day.
Said he, 'If you want,
We could share a croissant,'
For he'd heard about rolls in the hay.

Though his plan, when he gave her a buzz,
Was to do what man normally does,
She declared, 'I'm a Soul
Not a sexual goal!'
So he shrugged and called someone who was.

There was a young man named Houdini,
Who spilled some gin on his weenie.
So just to be couth,
He added vermouth,
Then slipped his girl a martini.

There was an old maid of Duluth
Who wept when she thought of her youth,
And the glorious chances
She'd missed at school dances,
And once in a telephone booth.

There was an old fellow named Paul
Whose prick was exceedingly small
When in bed with a lay
He could screw her all day
Without touching the vaginal wall.

There was a young fellow from Wark,
Who, when he screws, has to bark.
His wife is a bitch,
With a terrible itch,
So the town never sleeps after dark.

Strensall – Times Two.
1. There was a young fellow of Strensall,
Whose prick was as sharp as a pencil.
On the night of his wedding,
It went through the bedding,
And shattered the chamber utensil.

2. So here was this fellow from Strensall,
Whose pecker was shaped like a pencil,
Anemic, 'tis true,
But an interesting screw,
Inasmuch as the tip is prehensile.

There is a professor named Martin
From whom I'm about to be partin',
And on my way out,
He may here me shout,
'It's your face I'd sure like to fart in.'

There was a young student of Yale
Who was getting his first piece of tail.
He shoved in his pole,
But in the wrong hole,
And a voice from beneath yelled: 'No sale!'

There was a young lady of Exeter,
So pretty, that men craned their necks at her.
One was even so brave
As to take out and wave
The distinguishing mark of his sex at her.

A near-sighted chap named Coulter
Led a glamorous gal to the altar.
Quite lovely he thought her
Till strong soap and hot water
Made her look like the rock of Gibraltar.

There was a young fellow of Barrow,
Whose whang-bone was lacking in marrow.
To get some action
He put it in traction
And feathered the shaft like an arrow.

There was an old man from New York
Whose tool was as dry as a cork.
While attempting to screw,
He split it in two,
Now he uses the thing as a fork.

There once was a man from Australia
Who went on a wild bacchanalia.
He buggered a frog,
Two mice, and a dog,
And a bishop in fullest regalia.

A lesbian lady named Maud
Got into the WACs by a fraud
With a tongue long and knobby
She raped Colonel Hobby
And now she's a Major, by Gawd!

There was a young man with a fiddle
Who asked of his girl, 'Do you diddle?'
She replied, 'Yes, I do,
But prefer to with two.
It's twice as much fun in the middle.'

There was a young man up in Utah
Who constructed a condom of pewter.
He said, 'I confess
You feel nothing or less,
But it makes you as safe as a neuter.'

There was a young man of Bengal
Who swore he had only one ball,
But two little bitches
Unbuttoned his britches
And found he had no balls at all.

There once was a gay young Parisian
Who screwed an appendix incision,
And the girl of his choice
Could hardly rejoice
At this horrible lack of precision.

A medical student named Hetrick
Is learned in matters obstetric.
From a glance at the toes
Of a mother, he knows
If the new baby's balls are symmetric.

There's an over-sexed lady named Whyte
Who insists on a dozen a night.
A fellow named Cheddar
Had the brashness to wed her
His chance of survival is slight.

A young man whose sight was myopic
Thought sex an incredible topic.
So poor were his eyes,
That despite its great size,
His penis appeared microscopic.

There was a young lady of Wheeling
Who professed to lack sexual feeling.
But a cynic named Boris
Just touched her clitoris,
And she had to be scraped off the ceiling.

A school boy who thought he could fake 'um,
Told the doctor he felt a sharp ache come;
The X-ray applied
Showed all his inside
Was looking as well as they make 'um.

There Once was . . .

THE words 'There once was a boy/girl/man/woman/butcher
. . . named' is the classic opening line for the limerick.
Here are a few examples:

There once was a young boy named Steven
Who noticed his balls were uneven.
When he pulled on the right,
The left shot out of sight:
Not the effect Steve was keen on achievin'.

There once was a young man named Springer
Got his testicles caught in the wringer.
He hollered with pain,
As they rolled down the drain,
'There goes my career as a singer.'

There once was a girl called Honor
Who set a fire under Conner
He screamed out in fright
Called 'Put out the light!'
But my best friend called out 'Good on ya!'

There once was a girl named Miss Nokes,
Who showed her behind to the folks.
Everyone cheered,
And a vendor appeared
Selling hotdogs and popcorn and Cokes.

There once was a man named McChizes
Who had balls of various sizes.
One ball was so small,
It was no ball at all,
But the other big bastard won prizes.

There once was a man named Mort
Whose dick was incredibly short
He climbed into bed
And his lady friend said,
'That's not a dick, it's a wart.'

There once was a woman named Ann
Who was said to be quite like a man.
When nature did call,
She ran down the hall,
And went to the gentleman's can.

Women

There was a young lady named Sue
Who preferred a stiff drink to a screw.
But one leads to the other,
And now she's a mother
Let this be a lesson to you.

There was a young woman in Dee
Who stayed with each man she did see.
When it came to a test
She wished to be best,
And practice makes perfect, you see.

There was an old whore of Algiers
Who had bushels of dirt in her ears.
The tip of her titty
Was also quite gritty,
She never had washed it in years.

There was a young Queen of Baroda
Who built a new kind of pagoda.
The walls of its halls
Were festooned with the balls
And the tools of the fools that bestrode her.

An orgasm can be, oh, so fine.
A multiple one quite divine.
But if you should moan,
And it's not on your own,
Then you faked it, you bullshitting swine.

There was a young girl with a pretty-ass,
And her habits were neat but invidious.
She would wipe with a taper
Of scented blue paper,
Since she was so very fastidious.

An ignorant maiden named Crewe-Pitt
Did something amazingly stupid:
When her lover had spent
She douched with cement,
And gave birth to a statue of Cupid.

A big-breasted broad from Point Breeze
Once said to her lover, 'Oh please!
You'd enhance my bliss
If you'd play more with this
And pay less attention to these.'

'My body, by my own admission,'
I told him, 'Is in top condition.'
I said with a snigger,
'I worship my figure.'
Then he tried to embrace my religion.

Most all husbands can testify
To a wedding they cannot deny.
'Cause they know where and when
They got married, but then,
What exactly escapes them is why.

My back aches, my pussy is sore;
I simply can't screw any more
I'm covered with sweat
And you haven't come yet
And my God, it's a quarter to four!

I told her, 'Your bank account's knotted,
You've spent so much more than allotted.'
She said with a yawn,
'I'm not overdrawn,
It's just simply an under-deposit!'

There was a young lady of Spain
Who took down her pants on a train.
There was a young porter
Saw more than he orter,
And asked her to do it again.

There was a young lady named Clair
Who possessed a magnificent pair.
Or at least so I thought,
Till I saw one get caught
On a thorn, and began losing air.

There was a young lady called Valerie
Who started to count every calorie
Said her boss in disgust:
'If you lose half your bust
You'll be worth only half of your salary!'

There was a young girl from Hong Kong
Whose cervical cap was a gong.
She said with a yell,
As a shot rang her bell,
'I'll give you a ding for a dong!'

There was a young girl from New York
Who plugged her pussy with a cork.
A woodpecker or two
Made the grade, it is true,
But it totally baffled the stork.

There was a young lady named Gloria
Who was had by Sir Gerald Du Maurier,
And then by six men,
Sir Gerald again,
And the band at the Waldorf-Astoria.

There was a young lady from China,
Who had an enormous vagina
And when she was dead
They painted it red
And used it for docking a liner.

Said a horny young girl from Milpitas,
'My favourite sport is coitus.'
But a fullback from State
Made her period late
And now she has athlete's foetus

There was a young girl from China
Who stretched catgut across her vagina
From the lovemaking frock
With the proper sized cock
Came Toccata and Fugue in D Minor.

An overworked hooker once said,
'I must change the sheets on my bed.
I've developed a rash
On the lips of my gash
And the inside's all puffy and red.'

There once was a technician named Lil.
That took a nuclear pill.
They found her vagina
In South Carolina
And her boobs in a tree in Brazil!

Undressing a maiden called Sue,
Her seducer exclaimed, 'If it's true
That a nipple a day
Keeps the doctor away,
Think how healthy you must be with two!'

There was a young lady named Smith
Whose virtue was largely a myth
She said, 'Try as I can
I can't find a man
Who it's fun to be virtuous with.'

There was a young lady from Kew
Who filled her vagina with glue.
She said with a grin,
'If they pay to get in,
They will pay to get out of it, too.'

There was a young girl named Sapphire
Who succumbed to her lover's desire
She said, 'It's a sin,
But now that it's in
Could you shove it a few inches higher?'

An uptight young lady named Breerley
Who valued her morals too dearly
Had sex, so I hear,
Only once every year,
And she strained her vagina severely.

There once was a lady from France
Who took a long train ride by chance
The engineer f***ed her
Before the conductor
While the fireman came in his pants.

A handsome young widow named Vi
Seduced all the wardens nearby.
When the sirens said, 'Woo!'
What else could they do
To extinguish the gleam in her eye?

There once was a girl from Lahore
Who'd lie on a rug on the floor
In a manner uncanny,
She'd wiggle her fanny
And drain your balls to the core.

There was a young sailor from Brighton,
Who said 'Shit! Your hole is a tight one!'
Said the girl, 'Shut your face!
You're in the wrong place!
There's plenty of room in the right one!'

There was a young laundress named Wrangle
Whose tits tilted up at an angle.
'They may tickle my chin,'
She said with a grin,
'But at least they keep out of the mangle.'

There once was a harlot name Sumi
Whose pussy was not very roomy
Because of this
She was a popular Miss
And never once drove clients loony!

There was a young girl named Dalrymple
Whose sexual equipment was so simple,
That on examination they found
Little more than a mound
In the centre of which was a dimple.

There was an aesthetic young Miss
Who thought it the apex of bliss
To jazz herself silly
With the bud of a lily,
Then go to the garden and piss.

The Penis

A young man maintained that his trigger
Was so big that there weren't any bigger.
But this long and thick pud
Was so heavy it could
Scarcely lift up its head. It lacked vigour.

A man with a fever so dire,
Had testes which burned like a pyre.
He was heard to exclaim,
As they put out the flame,
'Goodness gracious, great balls of fire.'

There was an old man of Tagore
Whose tool was a yard long or more,
So he wore the damn thing
In a surgical sling
To keep it from wiping the floor.

Did you hear about young Henry Lockett?
He was blown down the street by a rocket.
The force of the blast
Blew his balls up his arse,
And his pecker was found in his pocket.

There once was a young man named McNamara
Who had a penis of prodigious diameter.
But it was not his size
That gave girls surprise,
It was his rhythm, iambic pentameter.

There was a young fellow of Harrow
Whose john was the size of a marrow.
He said to his tart,
'How's this for a start?
My balls are outside in a barrow.'

An old man who barely did kissing
Soon discovered what he'd been missing.
When laid down on the sod,
He cried out, 'Oh, my God!
All these years I just used it for pissing!'

There was a young man of Malacca
Who always slept on his left knacker.
One Saturday night
He slept on his right,
And his knacker went off like a cracker.

There was a young man whose dong
Was prodigiously, massively long
Down the sides of his whang,
Two testes did hang
Which attracted a curious throng.

All winter the eunuch from Munich
Went walking in naught but a tunic.
Folks said, 'You've a cough;
You'll freeze your balls off!'
He said, 'That's why I'm a eunuch.'

Floating idly one day through the air
A circus performer named Blair
Tied a sizeable rock
To the end of his cock
And shattered a balcony chair.

John's testicles groaned and said, 'Ouch!',
As he fondled young Jane on the couch.
Said the left, 'I feel blue';
Said the right one, 'Me too',
As they jiggled around in their pouch.

There was a young man in Hong Kong
Who grew seven fathoms of dong.
It looked, when erect,
About as you'd expect,
When coiled it did not seem so long.

A fussy young fellow named Lear
Used to wash off his bollocks with beer.
Said he, 'By the gods,
This is good for the cods
Look, they're full of good cheer.'

A farmer I know named O'Doul
Has a long and incredible tool.
He can use it to plough,
Or to diddle a cow,
Or just as a cue-stick at pool.

There once was a man from Madras
Whose balls were constructed of brass
When jangled together
They played Stormy Weather
And lightning shot out of his ass!

That wily old pervert St Nick
Made good use of the curve to his dick
He glazed the whole shaft
Painted stripes, then he laughed
As he offered young ladies a lick.

There was a young fellow named Paul
Who confessed, 'I have only one ball
But the size of my prick
Is God's dirtiest trick
For my girls always ask, 'Is that all?'

There was a young man of Devizes
Whose balls were of different sizes.
One was so small
It was nothing at all
The other took numerous prizes.

A lady while dining at Crewe
Found an elephant's whang in her stew
Said the waiter, 'Don't shout
And don't wave it about
Or the others will all want one too.'

The mate on the SS *Belgrave*
Didn't care for his God or his Saviour
He walked on the decks
Proudly waving his sex
And was bridged for indecent behaviour.

There was a young man from Salinas
Who had an extremely long penis:
Believe it or not,
When he lay on his cot
It reached from Marin to Martinez.

There was a young student from Boston
Who drove around in an Austin.
There was room for his ass
And a gallon of gas.
But his balls hung out and he lost 'em.

There once was a man from Kent,
Whose cock was so long it bent
To save him the trouble
He put it in double
And instead of coming he went.

There was an old gent from Kentucky
Who boasted a filigreed schmucky,
But he put it away
For fear that one day
He might put it in and get stucky.

There was a young fellow named Kimble
Whose prick was exceedingly nimble,
But fragile and slender,
And dainty and tender,
So he kept it encased in a thimble.

A young man, quite free with his dong,
Said the thing could be had for a song.
Such response did he get
That he rented the Met,
And held auditions all the day long.

The favourite pastime of grandfather
Was tickling his balls with a feather.
But the thing he liked best
Of all of the rest,
Was knocking them gently together.

Places

English Places

There once was a man from Great Britain
Who interrupted two girls at their knittin'.
Said he with a sigh,
'That park bench, well I
Just painted it right where you're sittin'.'

A cockeyed Old Cockney called Billy
Had ambitions misguided and silly,
He sat on the stairs,
Eating apples and pears,
Teaching rhyming slang, willy-nilly.

A shiftless young fellow of Kent
Had his wife love the landlord for rent.
But as she grew older
The landlord grew colder,
And now they live out in a tent.

There once was a man from St Paul,
Who moaned about being so tall.
At night, in his bed,
Was his body and head.
His feet had to sleep in the hall.

There was a young lady from Ealing
Whose kisses were warm and appealing.
If someone complained
Her passion was feigned
She'd kiss them again with more feeling.

There was a young girl from Oliver
And all the men did follow her
Until a guy came along
And played her his song
And all the rest quit call'n her.

There was a young colonel from Trent
Who lived in a lavender tent.
He said that some sessions
With interesting Hessians
Had taught him what war really meant.

There was a young girl from Cape Cod
Who thought babies came only from God.
'Twasn't the Almighty
Who lifted her nightie.
'Twas Roger the Lodger by god! the God.

There once was a lady from Hyde
Who ate a green apple and died
While her lover lamented
The apple fermented,
And made cider inside her inside.

There once was a man from York
Who picked his nose with a fork
But his face caved in
And it was impossible to grin
So he ended up looking like a dork.

There was a young man from Montrose
Who could diddle himself with his toes.
He did it so neat
He fell in love with his feet,
And christened them Myrtle and Rose.

Other Places

Said an Argentine gaucho named Bruno,
'Three things about morals I do know
Fornication's perverse;
Bestiality's worse;
And chastity's numero uno.'

That Man from Peru
Five verses

There one was a man from Peru
Who dreamed of eating his shoe
He awoke with a fright
In the middle of the night
And found that his dream had come true!

There once was a man from Peru
Who had a lot of growing up to do
He'd ring the doorbell
Then run off like hell
Until the owner shot him with a .22.

There once was a man from Peru
Who fell asleep in his canoe
While dreaming of Venus
He played with his penis
And woke up covered in goo.

There was an Old Man of Peru,
Who never knew what he should do;
So he tore out his hair,
And behaved like a Bear,
Till they carried him off to the Zoo.

There was a young man from Peru
Whose lineage was noble all through.
Now this isn't crud
For not only his blood
But even his semen was blue.

A proper young man from Ensay
Takes a young lady to lunch every day
He said, 'I admit
That her charm and her wit
Make it worth every penny I pay.'

A gay guy one time in Khartoum,
Asked a lesbian up to his room
They spent the whole night
In a hell of a fight
About which should do what, and to whom.

There was a young lady of Norway
Who hung by her heels in the doorway.
'Come look at me, Joe,'
She said real slow
'I think I have found yet one more way.'

There was a young man of Belgravia
Who decried God and his Saviour.
He walked down the Strand
With his balls in his hand,
And was had up for indecent behaviour.

There was an Old Person of Ischia
Whose conduct grew friskier and friskier
He danced hornpipes and jigs
And ate thousands of figs
'More whiskey!' he cried, 'Makes me riskier!'

There was an old maid from Bermuda
Who shot a marauding intruder.
It was not her ire
At his lack of attire,
But he reached for her jewels as he screwed her.

There once was a witch from St Rose,
Who hated the wart on her nose.
'I think you will find,
That true love is blind.'
Said her date, a gnome with three toes.

There was an old lady from Japan
Who sat on an old frying pan
She burnt her thumb
Her bottom went numb
But she'll do it again if she can.

In the Garden of Eden they dwelt;
And on his right knee, Adam knelt.
He said to his Eve,
'Do you really love me?'
And that's when she answered, 'Who else?'

There once was a maid in Duluth,
A striver and seeker of truth.
This pretty wench
Was adept at French,
And said all else was uncouth.

There was young man from Galosham
Who took out his knackers to wash 'em,
His wife said 'Jack,
If you don't put them back,
I'll jump on the buggers and squash em.'

There was a young lady from Plod
Who thought she was pregnant by God
But it wasn't the Almighty
That lifted her nightie
It was Roger the Lodger, the Sod.

There are variations of this limerick. See also the full version of The Farter from Sparta in the Toilet Humour section later in this chapter.

There was a young fellow from Sparta,
A really magnificent farter,
On the strength of one bean
He'd fart *God Save the Queen,*
And Beethoven's *Moonlight Sonata.*

There was a young fellow from Wark,
Who, when he screws, has to bark.
His wife is a bitch,
With a terrible itch,
So the town never sleeps after dark.

A greengrocer's girl from the Humber
The boys thought a really hot number.
When business was slow,
She'd put on a show,
Performing the cucumber rumba.

There was an old rake from Stamboul
Felt his ardour grow suddenly cool.
No lack of affection
Reduced his erection
But his zipper got caught in his tool.

There was an old man from New York
Whose tool was as dry as a cork.
While attempting to screw,
He split it in two,
Now he uses the thing as a fork.

There was a young man up in Utah
Who constructed a condom of pewter.
He said, 'I confess
You feel nothing or less,
But it makes you as safe as a neuter.'

A remarkable race are the Persians,
They have such peculiar diversions.
They screw the whole day
In the regular way,
And save up the nights for perversions.

There once was a handsome Haitian,
The luckiest man in creation.
He worked for the rubber trust
Teaching the upper crust
The science of safe copulation.

Near a shiny light beer can stood Dwight
Slyly dropping his trousers one night
In a bar in Rangoon
Pantomiming the tune
By the Moon of the Silvery Light . . .

The Vizier of Stamboul, a Turk,
Had an emerald hilt on his dirk.
But his dong set with rubies
Drove crazy the pubies
Of ladies who lightened his work.

There was a young lady from Wheeling
Who was out in the garden a-kneeling,
When by some strange chance
She got ants in her pants,
And invented Virginia reeling.

There once was a girl from Nigeria,
Who loved to eat foods with fiberia.
She ate cabbage and prunes,
And lots of legumes,
Now her husband lives in Siberia.

A pretty young girl Eskimo
Thought it very patriotic to sew
Bollock-warmers for those
Who were fighting the foes,
And on whom the North wind would blow.

There was an old girl in Havana
Who slipped on the skin of a banana,
Whoops! Went her feet,
And she fell on her seat,
In a most unladylike manner.

Another old lady named Hannah,
Slipped on that same darned banana,
As she lay on her side,
More stars she spied
Than there are in the 'Star-Spangled Banner'.

There was a young man from Aberdeen
Who invented a jerking machine.
On the twenty-fifth stroke
The goddamn thing broke
And beat his balls into a cream.

There was a young fellow of Perth
Whose balls were the finest on earth.
They grew to such size
That one won a prize,
And goodness knows what they were worth.

There was a young virgin in Perth
Swore she'd do it for no-one on earth,
Yet she fell without scandal
To a red Christmas candle
And was always less choosey henceforth.

There once was a fellow from Yuma,
Told an elephant joke to a puma.
Now his skeleton lies
Under hot western skies.
The Puma had no sense of huma!

A thrifty young fellow of Shoreham
Made brown paper trousers and wore 'em.
He looked nice and neat,
Till he bent in the street
To pick up a dime, then he tore 'em.

A pretty young maiden from France
Decided she'd 'just take a chance.'
She let herself go,
For an hour or so,
And now all her sisters are aunts.

A nudist resort at Buenos Aires
Took a midget in all unawares.
But he made members weep
For he just couldn't keep
His nose out of private affairs.

There once was a lady from Cadger
Who, as the result of a wager,
Consented to fart
The whole oboe part
Of Mozart's Quartet in F-Major.

I wooed a shrewd nude in Bermuda,
I was lewd, but my God! she was lewder.
She said it was crude
To be wooed in the nude
I pursued her, subdued her, and screwed her.

There once was a man from Deep River,
Who drank till he ruined his liver.
He'd drink, then he'd drive
He's no longer alive
And he ended his days all aquiver.

There once was a monk from Tibet,
Who said to a woman he met,
'You may find this odd,
But I'm One with God,
And HE wants to fondle your set!'

A Chester man sure loved his scotch. Oh,
He thought it made him feel so macho.
One night when he binged
He came really unhinged,
So now he drinks only gazpacho.

A farmer from out in Algiers,
Planted some corn in his ears.
When the temperature rose,
He leapt to his toes.
Now popping is all that he hears.

There once was a man from St Paul's
Who used to perform in the halls.
His favourite trick
Was to stand on his prick
And roll off the stage on his balls.

The Dick

10 Verses
There was a young fellow named Dick
Who perfected a wonderful trick:
With a safe for protection
He'd get an erection,
And then balance himself on his prick.

'Twas a fearful and wonderful sight,
And the ladies all shrieked with delight,
But the men were less zealous
For it made them all jealous,
And they said that it wasn't polite.

But that night each one tried it and failed,
While their wives looked on helpless and wailed,
For either they'd teeter
And fall on their peter,
Or they'd find themselves getting derailed.

So Dick was the toast of the town,
There was nothing too good for the clown,
And the wives all came flocking
To sample his cocking,
While the husbands deplored his renown.

Then along came a fellow from France
Whose success you'd foretell at a glance,
For his cock didn't dangle
But stayed at right angle,
Which gave him an excellent stance.

With a flourish he took off his clothes,
And assumed Dick's remarkable pose,
But the chief of his talents
Was keeping his balance
While he juggled his balls with his toes.

Then came the best part of all,
That always would bring down the hall,
For his finishing trick
Was to straddle his prick,
And wheel out of sight on one ball.

The ladies all ran and told Dick
That the Frenchman had bettered his trick,
So he straddled and struggled
And finally juggled,
But he knocked out his prop with a kick.

And the tragedy didn't end there,
For as he swirled down through the air
His prick became tied
In a knot that defied
All attempts to untangle its snare.

Most men would have died of remorse,
But Dick found another resource:
For pretzels he'd pose
With his twisted up hose,
And he made a nice income, of course.

Politics

In recent years, nothing has induced more aspiring wordsmiths to pen a limerick than the Clinton-Lewinsky affair.

There once was a gal named Lewinsky
Who played on a flute like Stravinsky
'Twas 'Hail to the Chief'
On this flute made of beef
That stole the front page from Kaczynski.

Said Bill Clinton to young Ms Lewinsky
We don't want to leave clues like Kaczynski,
Since you look such a mess,
Use the hem of your dress
And wipe that stuff off of your chinsky.

Lewinsky and Clinton have shown
What Kaczynski must surely have known:
That an intern is better
Than a bomb in a letter
Given the choice to be blown.

The president's loud protestation
On his fall to the intern's temptation
'This affair is still moral
As long as it's oral
Straight screwing I save for the nation.'

'Send the missiles!' Bill cried, 'On the double
Reduce those Afghanis to rubble.'
It made sense, he decided
His missile unguided
Was the thing that got him into trouble.

His eager young staffers all seek
To suck up the juice from his beak
Which is slightly perverse
But a thing that is worse
Is to swallow the words that he speaks.

At the White House, a young girl interned
And her passion for Slick Willie burned.
But her ardour soon cooled
As the media drooled
While by Slick she was publicly spurned!

There once was a leader from Hope
Who financed his elections with dope.
And then later he wailed
'I never inhaled
And I always thought hemp was just rope.'

The President swore to the sky
He'd never asked someone to lie
But the chance was then missed
To request that he list
Positions he'd told them to try.

Bill Clinton's no man of conviction,
Avoiding truth is a lifelong affliction.
Mixes lies with the facts,
We can never relax,
To him, truth IS stranger than fiction.

'Miss Jones,' Clinton said with affection,
'Be so kind as to check my erection.'
But Paula so silly
Misunderstood her Willy,
And thought he said, 'Wreck my election.'

A DA who'd just passed the bar
Told Monica, 'Come as you are
There's no need to dress
We don't want to mess
With evidence that you can show Starr.'

A right-wing spin doctor who's spun
Lurid tales about Monica's fun
Exclaimed when his eyes
Saw the fruit of his lies
'We've gotten O.J. off page one!'

The President having seen action
Thought he'd had full satisfaction
Then the news of the day
And an urge made him say
'I want to retract my retraction.'

They wanted to put Bill in jail
For using his house to chase tail
But the judge wasn't fooled
Saw no crime so he ruled
'Not guilty! He didn't inhale.'

All those Monica limericks are lame,
But I guess we have Clinton to blame.
Had he f***ed just his wife,
For once in his life,
Or at least missed the dress when he came.

But, as this one shows from more than half a century
ago, it's all happened before:

Said Senator David I. Walsh,
'These charges against me are false.
Though I did go to Brooklyn
For sooklyn and fooklyn,
Not a gob laid his hands on my balsh.'
1947

Two Ladies of Birmingham

Three Verses
1. There were two young ladies of Birmingham
And this is the story concerning 'em.
They lifted the frock
And diddled the cock
Of the Bishop while he was confirming 'em.

2. But the Bishop was nobody's fool,
He'd been to a large public school.
He dropped down his britches
And diddled those bitches
With his twelve-inch Episcopal tool.

3. But that didn't bother those two.
They said, as the Bishop withdrew:
'Oh the Vicar is quicker,
And thicker and slicker
And longer and stronger than you.'

Popular Culture

I am going out dancing tonight
With a couple of friends, to get tight,
If I come home all blurry
And sticky and slurry
And smelling of sick, don't take fright.

There was a young girl dressed in black,
Who kept her drugs in a spice rack.
It wasn't her fault,
Her mom thought it salt,
Now her family is all hooked on crack.

There once was a man named Ted
Who had pot growing out of his head.
The cause of those weeds
Was from smoking the seeds
Or so I have heard it been said.

You know that I like you a lot.
But I think you wish I did not.
So, I'll curb the emotion,
And end the devotion.
My life has such a bad plot.

A mean and odiferous punk
Ate Limberger cheese by the chunk.
Combined with BO,
And the farts that he'd blow,
It was worse than a run-over skunk.
An entrepreneur stuck with oodles
Of cans holding tofu and noodles
Scored a marketing coup
When he labelled them 'New!
Gourmet Delight for Toy Poodles.'

There was a young gambler named Brock,
Who ordered a bundle of stock.
The stockbroker fumbled;
The stockmarket tumbled,
And now Mr Brock is in hock.

There once was a girl from South Philly
Who quit Greenpeace 'cos she thought it was silly.

I said, 'Don't worry, Gail,
If you still want to pet a whale,
Just undo my zipper and Free Willy!'

Although watching TV is no plus
At the people who do it, don't fuss
We should never berate a
Complete couch potato
Especially Net nerds like us.

Roman Times

When Brutus, that jolly old teaser
Told a joke to a regal old geezer
In the shade of an arch
On the ides of March
'Tee hee, Brutus,' said Caesar.

The Services

A notorious hooker named Shore
Would allow horny sailors to score,
But employed every means
Of avoiding Marines
She was rotten, they claimed, to the Corps.

I lost my arm in the army,
I lost my leg in the navy,
I lost my balls
Over Niagara Falls,
And I lost my cock in a lady.

The spouse of a pretty young thing
Came home from the wars in the spring.
He was lame but he came
With his dame like a flame
A discharge is a wonderful thing.

A Marine sergeant named William Cox
Made confession, then died in the box.
His Fidelis was Semper,
He died of distemper,
But some said he'd died of the pox.

A company of Grenadier Guards
While traversing the park, formed in squads,
Saw two naked statues
At three-quarter part views,
Which perceptibly stiffened their rods.

A man in the battle of Aix
Had one nut and his cock shot his way,
But found out in this pickle
His nose could still tickle,
Though he might get the snuffles some day.

There was a young Royal Marine,
Who tried to fart 'God Save the Queen'.
When he reached the soprano
Out came only guano
And his britches weren't fit to be seen.

An innocent soldier named Stave
Was almost seduced by a WAVE.
But he's still a recluse
With all of his juice,
For he didn't know how to behave.

A girl from Shanghai had a ball
With the whole Eighth Army last fall.
She was screwed, with a smile,
Seven times every mile,
The full length of the Chinese Great Wall.

There was a young corporal named Kildare
Who was fondling a girl in a chair.
On the forty-third stroke,
The furniture broke,
And his gun went off in the air.

Sex

A fellow who slept with a whore,
Used a safe, but his pecker got sore.
Said he with chagrin,
'Selling these is a sin.'
Said the druggist, 'Caveat emptor.'

There was a young student of Yale
Who was getting his first piece of tail.
He shoved in his pole,
But in the wrong hole,
And a voice from beneath yelled: 'No sale!'

There was an old whore from Castile,
Whose favours were thought quite a deal.
But the men that she screws,
All start singing the blues
When their pricks start to blister and peel.

There was an old Sarge of Dorchester
Who invented a mechanical whore-tester.
With an electrical eye,
His tool, and a die,
He observed each sore pimple and fester.

Thus writes Lady Vanderbilt-Horsett,
Who invented the Lonely-Maid Corset:
'I thought all vicarious
F***ing precarious.
I was wrong. It's a whiz. I endorse it.'

In the Garden of Eden sat Adam
Massaging the bust of his madam
He chuckled with mirth,
For he knew that on earth
There were only two boobs and he had 'em.

A lonely young lad of Eton
Used always to sleep with the heat on,
Till he ran into a lass
Who showed him her ass
Now they sleep with only a sheet on.
1943

There once was a young man named Gene
Who invented a screwing machine
Concave and convex
It served either sex
And it played with itself in between.

There was a young lady quite mild
Who kept herself quite undefiled
By thinking of Jesus
Contagious diseases
And the bother of having a child.

On Viagra was old Charlie Muldoon,
When he went on his fifth honeymoon.
Monday coffee was brewing
When he started in screwing
And he finished the Thursday at noon.

There was a young lady from Thrace
Whose corsets grew too tight to lace.
Her mother said, 'Nelly,
There's more in your belly
Than ever went in through your face!'

There once was a maiden of Siam
Who said to her lover, 'Don't try 'em
If you kiss me, of course
You will have to use force,
But God knows you're stronger than I am.'

Here was a man who lived in the fort
Whose dick was unfortunately short
When he hopped into bed
His girlfriend said,
'Christ, that's no dick, it's a wart.'

Once a young fellow named Skinner
Took a lady to dinner to win her,
At a quarter past nine,
They started to dine,
At a quarter past ten, it was in her.

There was a young man of Cape Horn
Who wished he had never been born.
And he wouldn't have been
If his father had seen
That the end of the rubber was torn.

There was a young lady of Worcester
Who dreamt that a rooster seduced her
She woke with a scream
But 'twas only a dream
A lump in the mattress had goosed her.

There were three young maidens of Twickenham
Who wanted Tom, Harry, and Dick in 'em
They prayed hard to Venus
Saying, 'Surely, between us
We can lengthen, and strengthen, and thicken 'em.'

There was a young lady of Michigan,
Who said, 'Damn it! I've got the itch again.'
Said her mother, 'That's strange,
I'm surprised it ain't mange,
If you've slept with that son-of-a-bitch again.'

A sexy young maiden named Jill
Tried a dynamite stick for a thrill
They found her vagina
In North Carolina
And bits of her tits in Brazil.

A wicked old fellow named Jones
Would ring people up on their phones
And suggest with a grin
'Let us take off our skin
And converse on our phones in our bones.'

Sport

There was a swimmer from Toledo
Who strained as he put on his Speedo.
He finally succeeded,
But later conceded,
'The damn thing, it kills my libido!'

A golfer named Sandy MacFarr
Went to bed with a Hollywood star
When he first saw her gash he
Cried, 'Quick, goot muh mashie!
Uh thunk uh c'n muk it in par.'

There young lady golfer named Duff.
With a lovely, luxuriant muff.
In his haste to get in her,
One eager beginner
Lost both his balls in the rough.

A gigantic young crewman named Tate
Has a pecker whose weight is so great
That his dates fear to screw.
What's a stroke oar to do?
He's reduced to just pulling his weight.

They say that ex-president Taft
When hit by a golf ball, once laughed
And said, 'I'm not sore,
But although he called 'Fore'
The place where he hit me was aft.

There's a sports-minded co-ed named Sue
Who's been coxing the varsity crew.
In the shell, Sue is great,
But her boyfriend's irate
When she calls out the stroke as they screw.

There was a young man from Venice
Who played a good game of lawn tennis.
But the game he liked best,
Far more than the rest,
Was played with two balls and a pennis ...

An old bush walker named Campbell
Got tangled one day in a bramble.
He cried, 'Ouch, how it sticks!
But so many sharp pricks
Are not met everyday on a ramble.'

On the Margin . . .

A young man whose sight was myopic
Thought sex an incredible topic.
So poor were his eyes,
That despite its great size,
His penis appeared microscopic.

With his Asperger's Syndrome he coped
Quite as well as his doctors had hoped:
He hollowed a tree,
Moved in, and said, 'Me?
I'll go out no more, unless doped!'

An unfortunate lad from Madrid
Had both Super Ego and Id,
So whether he screwed,
Or completely eschewed,
He felt guilty, whatever he did.

Though treated in every known way,
His spirochetes grow day by day,
He's developed paresis,
Converses with Jesus,
And thinks he's the Queen of the May.

There was a young pansy named Gene
Who cruised a sadistic Marine.
Said the man with a smirk
As they got down to work,
'In this game the Jack beats the Queen.'

An erotic neurotic named Syd
Got his Ego confused with his Id.
His errant libido
Was like a torpedo,
And that's why he done what he did.

Two fairies were flitting one day
In the meadow where they liked to play,
When the male made a pass
At the other (a lass),
Showing not quite all fairies are gay.

A sensitive fellow named Harry
Thought sex too revolting to marry.
So he went out in curls
And frowned on the girls,
And he got to be known as a fairy.

There once was a well-groomed young nance
Who responded to every advance,
But rather than strip
He let anything slip
Through a hole in the seat of his pants.

Lisped a limp-wristed cowboy named Fay,
'It's a hell of a place to be gay!
I must, on these prairies,
Due to a shortage of fairies,
With the deer and the antelope play!'

A certain young person of Ghent,
Uncertain if lady or gent,
Shows his organs at large
For a small handling charge
To assist him in paying the rent.

Goodness gracious, egad
I think I've gone quite mad
I'm loopy I am
I'll use this battering ram
And I run around scantily clad.

A beat schizophrenic said, 'Me?
I am not I, I'm a tree.'
But another, more sane,
Shouted, 'I'm a Great Dane!'
And covered his pants leg with pee.

An epileptic from an interment camp
Was seduced on her couch by a tramp
But the first time he squeezed her
She had a grand seizure
And broke both his balls and a lamp.

There was a young lady whose eyes,
Were different as to colour and size
When she opened them wide
People all turned aside
And started away in surprise.

There was a young fellow named Dale
Who was hardly what you could call male.
His libido wasn't channelized
So he got psychoanalysed,
And now he can't get enough tail.

There was a young lady named Grace
Who had eyes in a very odd place
She could sit on the hole
Of a mouse or a mole
And stare the beast square in the face.

There lives a man in Calcutta
Who has a terrible stutter
When he asks for the bread
They will pass him instead
Beer, broccoli, beans, and the butter.

Toilet Humour

A sparkling young farter from Sparta,
His fart for no money would barter.
He could roar from his rear
Any scene from Shakespeare,
Or Gilbert and Sullivan's Mikado.

There was a young girl of La Plata
Who was widely renowned as a farter.
Her deafening reports
At the Argentine sports
Made her much in demand as a starter.

There was a young fellow of Chiselhurst
Who never could piss till he'd whistled first.
One evening in June
He lost track of the tune,
Dum-da-da-dee . . . and his bladder burst!

There was a young lady of Purdbright
Who never could quite get her turd right.
She'd go to the closet
And leave a deposit
Like a mouse or a bat or a bird might.

There once was a man named MacBride
Who fell in a privy and died.
He had a young brother,
Who fell in another,
And now they're interred (in turd) side by side.

There was a young man had the art
Of making a capital tart
With a handful of shit,
Some snot and a spit,
And he'd flavour the whole with a fart.
1879

There was a young fellow from Leeds
Who swallowed a package of seeds.
Great tufts of grass
Sprouted out of his ass
And his balls were all covered with weeds.

A certain young lady named Rowell
Had a musical bent to her bowel.
With a good plate of beans
Tucked under her jeans
She could play To A Wild Rose by MacDowell.
1947

There was a young lady named Rose
Who'd occasionally straddle a hose,
And parade about squirting
And spouting and spurting,
Pretending she pissed like her beaux.

When I was young and had no sense
I had a piss on an electric fence
It tickled me prick and shivered me balls
And made me shit me overalls
I needed biological war defence.

A hermit who had an oasis
Thought it the best of all places:
He could pray and be calm
'Neath a pleasant date palm,
While the lice on his ballocks ran races.

There was a young man of Australia
Who painted his bum like a dahlia.
The drawing was fine
The colour divine
But the scent – ah! that was a failure.

I once took the vicar to tea;
It was just as I thought it would be
His rumblings abdominal
Were simply phenomenal
And everyone thought it was me.

I dined with the Duchess of Lee,
Who asked: 'Do you fart when you pee?'
I said with some wit:
'Do you belch when you shit?'
And felt it was one up for me.

There was a young man of Loch Levin
Who went for a walk about seven.
He fell into a pit
That was brimful of shit,
And now the poor beggar's in heaven.

There was a young man named Cattell
Who knew psychophysics so well,
That each time he shit
He'd stop, measure it,
Its length, and its breadth, and its smell.

He could vary, with proper persuasion,
His fart to suit any occasion.
He could fart like a flute,
Like a lark, like a lute,
This highly fartistic Caucasian.

There was a young Scotchman named Jock
Who had a most horrible shock:
He once took a shit
In a leaf-covered pit,
And the crap sprung a trap on his cock.

There was a young fellow of Ealing,
Devoid of all delicate feeling.
When he read on the door:
'Don't shit on the floor'
He jumped up and shat on the ceiling.

There was a young man from Montmarte
Who was famed far and wide for his fart.
When they said, 'What a noise!'
He replied with great poise,
'When I fart, sir, I fart from the heart.'

Woe, alack, and alas!
I'm held together by intestinal gas!
Each time I fart,
Something falls apart.
See! There's a crack in my ass!

There was a young man of Rangoon
Whose farts could be heard on the moon.
When least you'd expect 'em,
They'd burst from his rectum
With the force of a raging typhoon.

A man from Southern Nantucket
Took a shit in a big rusty bucket.
He got wedged in that pail,
An embarrassing tale
It was only a fart that unstuck it.

There was an old fellow of Pittwood
Who never was able to shit good.
He'd leave small deposits
On shelves and in closets,
As a very small pup or a kit would.

A tender young schoolboy named Bart
Once silently squeezed out a fart.
The smell of his gas
Filled the entire math class
Then drifted to Music and Art.

The illustrious author, Dean Howells,
Had a terrible time with his bowels.
His wife, so they say,
Cleaned them out everyday
With special elongated trowels.

There was a young man named McBride
Who could fart whenever he tried.
In a contest he blew
Two thousand and two,
And then shit and was disqualified.

The Farter from Sparta

10 verses
A sparkling young farter from Sparta,
His fart for no money would barter.
He could roar from his rear
Any scene from Shakespeare,
Or Gilbert and Sullivan's Mikado.

He'd fart a gavotte for a starter,
And fizzle a fine serenata.
He could play on his anus
The Coriolanus:
Oof, boom, er-tum, tootle, yum tah-dah!

He was great in the Christmas Cantata,
He could double-stop fart the Toccata,
He'd boom from his ass
Bach's B-Minor Mass,
And in counterpoint, La Traviata.

Spurred on by a very high wager
With an envious German named Bager,
He'd proceeded to fart
The complete oboe part
Of a Hayden Octet in B-Major.

His repertoire ranged from classics to jazz,
He achieved new effects with bubbles of gas.
With a good dose of salts
He could whistle a waltz
And range from falsetto to bass.

His basso profundo with timbre so rare
He rendered quite often, with power to spare.
But his great work of art,
His fortissimo fart,
He saved for the Marche Militaire.

One day he was dared to perform
The William Tell Overture Storm,
But naught could dishearten
Our spirited Spartan,
For his fart was in wonderful form.

It went off in capital style,
And he farted it through with a smile,
Then, feeling quite jolly,
He tried the finale,
Blowing double-stopped farts all the while.

The selection was tough, I admit,
But it did not dismay him one bit,
Then, with ass thrown aloft
He suddenly coughed,
And collapsed in a shower of shit.

His bunghole was blown back to Sparta,
Where they buried the rest of our farter,
With a gravestone of turds
Inscribed with the words:
'To the Fine Art of Farting, A Martyr.'
1938

Traditional

A bather whose clothing was strewed
By breezes that left her quite nude
Saw a man come along
And, unless I'm quite wrong
You expected this line to be rude . . .

A notorious whore named Miss Hearst
In the weakness of men is well-versed.
Reads a sign o'er the head
Of her well-rumpled bed:
'The customer always comes first.'

In a castle that had a deep moat
Lived a chicken, a duck and a goat.
They wanted to go out
And wander about
But all they needed was a boat.

To his clubfooted child spoke Lord Gillity,
'Despite breeding from higher nobility
A recessive gene pair
In which we both parents share
Has challenged your pedal mobility.'

There was an Old Man in a boat
Who said 'I'm afloat! I'm afloat!'
When they said, 'No you ain't!'
He was ready to faint,
As the water came up to his throat.

There once was a midget named Carr
Who couldn't reach up to the bar,
So in every saloon
He climbed a spittoon
And guzzled his liquor from thar.

Said Old Father William, 'I'm humble,
And getting too old for a tumble,
But produce me a blonde,
And I'm still not beyond,
An attempt at an interesting fumble.'

I wonder what Christmas will be
No merriment, good cheer or glee
Now that Santa's arrested
Because someone protested
That he laid some doll under their tree.

Old Mother Hubbard
Went to the cupboard
To get her poor doggie a bone
When she bent over, young Rover took over
And gave her a bone of his own.

Jack and Jill went up the hill,
To smoke some marijuana,
Jack got high,
Pulled down his fly,
And asked Jill if she wanna.
Jill said yes,
Pulled up her dress,
And had a little fun,
But stupid Jill,
Forgot the pill,
And now they have a son.

There is an old hermit named Dave,
Who keeps a dead mower in his cave.
Since he can't cut the grass,
Now it's up to his ass.
(His donkey, you censors; behave!)

No matter how grouchy you're feeling,
You'll find the smile more or less healing.
It grows in a wreath
All around the front teeth
Thus preserving the face from congealing.

There was a horny goat lived on a hill,
So full of mischief, he let some spill.
He fast knocked Jack down
And broke the lad's crown,
But was a trite more attentive to Jill.

19th-Century Limericks

Talking or writing about sex is certainly no modern-day phenomenon. As far back as 1870, the limerick had begun to veer into the world of sex and used words that were not heard in social circles of the times, as these limericks, all written in the supposedly prudish Victorian times, reveal.

Where possible, the date that each limerick first began to circulate is shown below the fifth line.

There was an old lady from Wheeling
Who had a peculiar feeling,
She laid on her back
And opened her crack
And pissed all over the ceiling.
1870

There was a young woman of Norway
Who drove a rare trade in the whore way,
Till a sodomite Viscount
Brought c*** to a discount,
And the bawdy house belles to a poor way.
1870

There was a young lady of Lincoln
Who said that her c*** was a pink'un,
So she had a prick lent her
Which turned it magenta,
This artful old lady of Lincoln.
1870

There was an old man of Ramnugger
Who drove a rare trade as a bugger,
Till a fair young Circassian
Brought f***ing in fashion,
And spoilt all the trade in Ramnugger.
1870

There was a young girl of Uttoxeter,
And all the young men shook their cocks at her.
From one of these cocks
She contracted the pox,
Now she's poxed all the cocks in Uttoxeter.
1870

A boy whose skin long I suppose is,
Was dreadfully ill with phimosis.
The doctor said, 'Why,
Circumcision we'll try,
A plan recommended by Moses.'
1870

There was an old man of Kentucky,
Said to his old woman, 'Oi'll f*** ye.'
She replied, 'Now you wunt
Come nigh my old c***,
For your prick is all stinking and mucky'.
1870

A youth who seduced a poor lighterman,
Said, 'I'd much sooner f*** than I'd fight a man,
And although, Sir, I find
You a very poor grind,
I must say I've had a much tighter man.'
1870

A Biblical party called Ham
Cried, 'Cuss it, I don't give a damn!
My father's yard measure
I view with great pleasure,
Such a bloody great battering ram!'
1870

There was an old Warden of Wadham, he
Was very much given to sodomy,
But he shyly confessed,
'I like tongue-f***ing best,
God bless my soul, isn't it odd of me?'
1870

There was a young lady of Lee
Who scrambled up into a tree,
When she got there
Her arsehole was bare,
And so was her see-you-en-t.
1870

There were three ladies of Huxham,
And whenever we meets 'em we f***s 'em,
And when that game grows stale
We sits on a rail,
And pulls out our pricks and they sucks 'em.
1870

There was a young lady called Tucker,
And the parson he tried hard to f*** her.
She said, 'You gay sinner,
Instead of your dinner,
At my c*** you shall have a good suck-ah.'
1870

There was a young lady of Dee
Who went down to the river to pee.
A man in a punt
Put his hand on her c***,
And God! how I wish it was me.
1870

There was a young lady of Ealing
And her lover before her was kneeling.
She said, 'Dearest Jim,
Take your hand off my quim,
I much prefer f***ing to feeling.'
1870

There was an old parson of Lundy,
Fell asleep in his vestry on Sunday.
He awoke with a scream:
'What, another wet dream!
This comes of not frigging since Monday.'
1879

There was an Old Man of the Mountain
Who frigged himself into a fountain
Fifteen times had he spent,
Still he wasn't content,
He simply got tired of the counting.
1879

There was a young lady of Gloucester
Whose friends they thought they had lost her,
Till they found on the grass
The marks of her ass,
And the knees of the man who had crossed her.
1870

A cheerful old party of Lucknow
Remarked, 'I should just like a f*** now!'
So he had one and spent
And said, 'I'm content,
By no means am I so c***-struck now.'
1879

There was a young man of Bulgaria
Who once went to piss down an area.
Said Mary to cook
'Oh, do come and look,
Did you ever see anything hairier?'
1880

Here's to it, and through it, and to it again,
To suck it, and screw it, and screw it again!
So in with it, out with it,
Lord work his will with it!
Never a day we don't do it again!
1880

There was a young widow of Nain
Who the bedclothes did frequently stain,
With such great inflammation
Came such menstruation,
Her c*** so long idle had lain.
1870

There was a young sailor from Brighton
Who remarked to his girl, 'You're a tight one.'
She replied, ''Pon my soul,
You're in the wrong hole;
There's plenty of room in the right one.'
1882

There was a young girl of Blackheath
Who frigged an old man with her teeth.
She complained that he stunk
Not so much from the spunk,
But his arsehole was just underneath.
1870

There was a strong man from Drumrig
Who one day did ten times frig.
He buggered three sailors,
Four Jews and two tailors,
And ended by f***ing a pig.
1879

There was a young parson of Goring
Who made a small hole in the flooring.
He lined it all round,
Then laid on the ground,
And declared it was cheaper than whoring.
1879

There was a young man of Rangoon
Who farted and filled a balloon.
The balloon went so high
That it stuck in the sky,
And stank out the Man in the Moon.
1879

There was an old person of Sark
Who buggered a pig in the dark.
The swine, in surprise,
Murmured, 'God blast your eyes,
Do you take me for Boulton or Park?'
1879

A rank whore, there ne'er was a ranker,
Possessed an Hunterian chancre,
But she made an elision
By a transverse incision,
For which all her lovers may thank her.
1870

There was a young man of Berlin
Whom disease had despoiled of his skin,
But he said with much pride,
'Though deprived of my hide,
I can still enjoy a put in.'
1879

There was an old party of Wokingham.
And his whores said he always was poking 'em.
But all he could do
Was to tongue-f*** a few.
And sniff at his fingers while roking 'em.
1870

There was a young lady of Gaza
Who shaved her c*** clean with a razor.
The crabs in a lump
Made tracks to her rump,
Which proceeding did greatly amaze her.
1879

There was an old lady of Cheadle
Who sat down in church on a needle.
The needle, though blunt,
Penetrated her c***,
But was promptly removed by the beadle.
1879

A convict once, out in Australia,
Said unto his turnkey, 'I'll tail yer.'
But he said, 'You be buggered,
You filthy old sluggard,
You're forgetting as I am your jailer.'
1870

There was an old man of Molucca
Who wanted his daughter, to f*** her.
But she got the best
Of his little incest,
And poxed the old man of Molucca.
1870

There was a young lady of Lee
Who scrambled up into a tree,
When she got there
Her arsehole was bare,
And so was her c-u-n-t.
1870

Limericks 1900–1930

From the turn of the century through to the Depression, the relationship between sex and the limerick continued to develop, drawing on sources, locations and ideas from all over the world.

There was a young woman from Aenos
Who came to our party as Venus.
We told her how rude
'Twas to come there quite nude,
And we brought her a leaf from the green-h'us.
1907

Down in Berne, Minister Grew,
There's nothing that fellow won't screw,
From queens down to cooks
They're all on his books,
And he dabbles in sodomy, too.
1923

Alas for the Countess d'Isere,
Whose muff wasn't furnished with hair.
Said the Count, 'Quelle surprise!'
When he parted her thighs;
'Magnifique! Pourtant pas de la guerre.'
1926

There was a young man of Ostend
Who let a girl play with his end.
She took hold of Rover,
And felt it all over,
And it did what she didn't intend.
1927

There was a young girl named McKnight
Who got drunk with her boyfriend one night.
She came to in bed
With a split maidenhead,
That's the last time she ever was tight.
1927

There was a young fellow named Louvies
Who tickled his girl in the boovies,
And as she contorted,
He looked down and snorted,
'My prick wants to get in your movies!'
1927

There was a young man named McGurk
Who dozed off one night after work,
He had a wet dream
And awoke with a scream
Just in time to give it a jerk.
1927

There was a young lady of Twickenham
Who thought men had not enough prick in 'em.
On her knees every day
To God she would pray
To lengthen and strengthen and thicken 'em.
1927

There was a young man from South Wales
Who lived on clap juice and snails.
When he tired of these
He lived upon cheese
From his prick, which he picked with his nails.
1927

There was a young woman of Croft
Who played with herself in a loft,
Having reasoned that candles
Could never cause scandals,
Besides which they did not go soft.
1927

There was a young lady named May
Who frigged herself in the hay.
She bought a pickle,
One for a nickel,
And wore all the warts away!
1927

There was a young girl named Anheuser
Who said that no man could surprise her.
But Pabst took a chance,
Found Schlitz in her pants,
And now she is sadder Budweiser.
1927

When she wanted a new way to futter
He greased her behind with butter;
Then, with a sock,
In went his jock,
And they carried her home on a shutter.
1927

A tidy young lady of Streator
Dearly loved to nibble a peter.
She always would say,
'I prefer it this way.
I think it is very much neater.'
1927

There was an old fellow from Roop
Who'd lost all control of his poop.
One evening at supper
His wife said, 'Now, Tupper,
Stop making that noise with your soup!'
1927

There once was a man named Enus
Who had a 50 foot penis.
It dragged on the ground,
And made a bad sound,
And when stiff it reached up to Venus.

There was a young lady of Wheeling
Said to her beau, 'I've a feeling
My little brown jug
Has need of a plug',
And straightway she started peeling.
1927

There was a young girl of East Lynne
Whose mother, to save her from sin,
Had filled up her crack
To the brim with shellac,
But the boys picked it out with a pin.
1927

The young things who frequent picture palaces
Have no use for this psycho-analysis.
And although Doctor Freud
Is distinctly annoyed
They cling to their old-fashioned fallacies.
1927

There was a young fellow named Charteris
Put his hand where his young lady's garter is.
She said, 'I don't mind,
And up higher you'll find
The place where my f***er and farter is.'
1927

There was an old man of Decatur,
Took out his red-hot pertater.
He tried at her dent,
But when his thing bent,
He got down on his knees and he ate 'er.
1927

Pet snakes

Said a lovely young lady named Lake,
Pervertedly fond of a snake,
'If my good friend, the boa,
Shoots spermatozoa,
What offspring we'll leave in our wake!'

Another young lady would make
Advances to snake after snake.
Though men she had met
Got her diaphragm wet,
She wanted her glottis to shake.
1928

* * *

There was a young mate of a lugger
Who took out a girl just to hug her.
'I've my monthlies,' she said,
'And a cold in my head,
But my bowels work well . . . do you bugger?'
1928

There was a young man of Bengal
Who went to a fancy dress ball.
Just for a stunt
He dressed up as a c***
And was f***ed by a dog in the hall.
1928

There was a young man of Peru
Who dreamt he was had by a Jew.
He woke up at night
In a hell of a fright,
And found it was perfectly true.
1928

There once was a Hooker named Sue
Who filled her vagina with glue
She said with a grin
If they paid to get in
They'll pay to get out of it too!

There was an old girl of Kilkenny
Whose usual charge was a penny.
For the half of that sum
You could finger her bum,
A source of amusement to many.
1928

There was a young girl of Pitlochry
Who was had by a man in a rockery.
She said, 'Oh! You've come
All over my bum;
This isn't a f***- - - it's a mockery.'
1928

Two Verses . . .

There was a young man of Datchet
Who cut off his prick with a hatchet.
Then very politely
He sent it to Whitely,
And ordered a c*** that would match it.
1926

The Reply

'There is a young girl here at Vassar
And none, for your needs, could surpass her.
But she cannot detach it
And much less dispatch it.
You'll still have to bach it. Alas, sir!'
1927
*****

There once was a man of Geneva
Who buggered a black bitch retriever.
The result was a sow,
Two horses, a cow,
Three lambs and a London coal-heaver.
1930

There was a young lady from Slough
Who said that she didn't know how.
Then a young fellow caught her
And jolly well taught her;
She lodges in Pimlico now.
1928

There was an old man from near here,
Got awfully drunk upon beer.
He fell in a ditch
And a son of a bitch
Of a bulldog f***ed him in the ear.
1928

There once was a Vassar BA
Who pondered the problem all day
Of what there would be
If C-*-*-*
Were divided by C-O-C-K.
1928

A young PhD passing by,
She gave him the problem to try.
He worked the division
With perfect precision,
And the answer was B-A-B-Y.
1928

There was a young girl of Aberystwyth
Who took grain to the mill to get grist with.
The miller's son, Jack,
Laid her flat on her back,
And united the organs they pissed with.
1927

There was a young maid of Klepper
Went out one night with a stepper,
And now in dismay
She murmurs each day,
'His pee-pee was made of red-pepper!'
1927

There was a young fellow, a banker,
Had bubo, itch, pox, and chancre.
He got all the four
From a dirty old whore,
So he wrote her a letter to thank her.
1911

There was a young lady called Wylde
Who kept herself quite undefiled
By thinking of Jesus,
Contagious diseases,
And the bother of having a child.
1927

There was a young girl of Bombay
Who was put in the family way
By the mate of a lugger,
An ignorant bugger
Who always spelled c*** with a K.
1927

There was an old man who could piss
Through a ring and, what's more, never miss.
People came by the score,
And bellowed, 'Encore!
Won't you do it again, Sir? Bis! Bis!'
1928

There was a young curate of Buckingham
Who was blamed by the girls for not f***ing 'em.
He said, 'Though my cock
Is as hard as a rock,
Your c***s are too slack. Put a tuck in 'em.'
1928

There was a young man from Lynn
Whose cock was the size of a pin.
Said his girl with a laugh
As she felt his staff,
'This won't be much of a sin.'
1927

There was a young girl from the Creek
Who had her periods twice every week.
'How very provoking,'
Said the Vicar from Woking,
'There's no time for poking, so to speak.'
1927

There was a young man of St John's
Who wanted to bugger the swans.
But the loyal hall-porter
Said, 'Pray, take my daughter!
Them birds are reserved for the dons.'
1928

There were three young ladies of Grimsby
Who said, 'Of what use can our quims be?
The hole in the middle
Is so we can piddle,
But for what can the hole in the rims be?'
1928

Remember those two of Aberystwyth
Who connected the things that they pissed with?
She sat on his lap
But they both had the clap,
And they cursed with the things that they kissed with.
1928

There was a young man of Eau Claire
Who had an affair with a bear,
But the surly old brute
With a snap of her snoot
Left him only one ball and some hair.
1927

There was a young lady named Flynn
Who thought fornication a sin,
But when she was tight
It seemed quite all right,
So everyone filled her with gin.
1927

A young Juliet of St Louis
On a balcony stood, acting screwy.
Her Romeo climbed,
But he wasn't well timed,
And half-way up, off he went . . . blooey!
1927

There was a young girl of Spitzbergen
Whose people all thought her a virgin,
Till they found her in bed
With her quim very red,
And the head of a kid just emergin'.
1928

There was a young woman of Chester
Who said to the man who undressed her,
'I think you will find
That it's better behind . . .
The front is beginning to fester.'
1927

Limericks 1930–1960

Some amazing images were developed, as this vast selection
across three decades shows.

When a girl, young Elizabeth Barrett
Was found by her ma in a garret.
She had shoved up a diamond
As far as her hymen,
And was ramming it home with a carrot.
1932

There was a young fellow named Tucker
Who, instructing a novice cock-sucker,
Said, 'Don't bow out your lips
Like an elephant's hips,
The boys like it best when you pucker.'
1934

A sweet young strip dancer named Jane
Wore five inches of thin cellophane.
When asked why she wore it
She said, 'I abhor it,
But my juices would spatter like rain.'
1934

There was a young Sapphic named Anna
Who stuffed her friend's c*** with banana,
Which she sucked bit by bit
From her partner's warm slit,
In the most approved lesbian manner.
1934

There was a young priest named Delaney
Who said to the girls, 'Nota bene,
I've seen how you swish up
Your shirts at the bishop
Whenever the weather is rainy.'
1937

There was a young man of Jaipur
Whose cock was shot off in the war.
So he painted the front
To resemble a c***,
And set himself up as a whore.
1938

There was a young man from Rangoon
Who was born at least three months too soon.
He hadn't the luck
To be born of a f***,
But was shovelled in cold on a spoon.
1938

'I once knew a harlot named Sue,
And a versatile girl she was, too.
After ten years of whoredom
She perished of boredom
When she married a jackass like you!'
1938

There was a young girl from New York
Who diddled herself with a cork.
It stuck in her vagina,
Can you imagina
Prying it out with a fork!
1938

There was a young lady whose mind
Was never especially refined.
She got on her knees,
Her lover to please,
Who stuck in his prick from behind.
1939

A Plumber whose name was Ten Brink
Plumbed the cook as she bent o'er the sink.
Her resistance was stout,
And Ten Brink petered out
With his pipe-wrench all limber and pink.
1942

Seven Parts About Syphilis

There was a young man of Back Bay
Who thought syphilis just went away,
And felt that a chancre
Was merely a canker
Acquired in lascivious play.

Now first he got acne vulgaris,
The kind that is rampant in Paris,
It covered his skin,
From forehead to shin,
And now people ask where his hair is.

With symptoms increasing in number,
His aorta's in need of a plumber,
His heart is cavorting,
His wife is aborting,
And now he's acquired a gumma.

Consider his terrible plight,
His eyes won't react to the light,
His hands are apraxic,
His gait is ataxic,
He's developing gun-barrel sight.

His passions are strong, as before,
But his penis is flaccid, and sore,
His wife now has tabes
And sabre-shinned babies.
She's really worse off than a whore.

There are pains in his belly and knees,
His sphincters have gone by degrees,
Parozysmal incontinence,
With all its concomitants,
Brings on quite unpredictable pees.

Though treated in every known way,
His spirochetes grow day by day,
He's developed paresis,
Converses with Jesus,
And thinks he's the Queen of the May.
1938

There was a young man with one foot
Who had a very long root.
If he used this peg
As an extra leg
Is a question exceedingly moot.
1939

There was a young man from Nantucket
Who had such a big cock he could suck it.
He looked in the glass
And saw his own ass,
And broke his neck trying to f*** it.
1939

A young strong boxer named Louis,
Buggered a dastardly Jewess,
He said with a sigh
As his engine went dry,
'I wonder where all of my goo is?'
1939

There was a young fellow of Burma
Whose betrothed had good reason to murmur.
But now that he's married he's
Been using cantharides
And the root of their love is much firmer.
1939

A king sadly said to his queen,
'In parts you have grown far from lean.'
'I don't give a damn,
You've always liked ham,'
She replied, and he gasped, 'How obscene!'
1943

The Shah of the Empire of Persia
Lay for days in a sexual merger.
When the nautch asked the Shah,
'Won't you ever withdraw?'
He replied with a yawn, 'It's inertia.'
1938

A nudist by name Roger Peet,
Loved to dance in the snow and the sleet,
But one chilly December
He froze every member,
And retired to a monkish retreat.
1939

There was a young man in Norway,
Tried to jerk himself off in a sleigh,
But the air was so frigid
It froze his balls rigid,
And all he could come was frappe.
1938

Double Trouble

Three verses

There was a young lady of Natchez
Who chanced to be born with two snatches,
And she often said, 'Shit!
Why, I'd give either tit
For a man with equipment that matches.'

There was a young fellow named Locke
Who was born with a two-headed cock.
When he'd fondle the thing
It would rise up and sing
An antiphonal chorus by Bach.

But whether these two ever met
Has not been recorded as yet,
Still, it would be diverting
To see him inserting
His whang while it sang a duet.
1939

There was a young man from Stamboul
Who boasted so torrid a tool
That each female crater
Explored by his satyr
Seemed almost unpleasantly cool.
1939

Oh, pity the Duchess of Kent!
Her c*** is so dreadfully bent,
The poor wench doth stammer,
'I need a sledgehammer
To pound a man into my vent.'
1939

There was a young lady of Chichester
Who made all the saints in their niches stir.
One morning at matins
Her breasts in white satins
Made the Bishop of Chichester's britches stir.
1939

There once was a girl from Cornell
Whose teats were shaped like a bell.
When you touched them they shrunk,
Except when she was drunk,
And then they got bigger than hell.
1939

Coitus upon a cadaver
Is the ultimate way you can have 'er.
Her inanimate state
Means a man needn't wait,
And eliminates all the palaver.
1940

There was a young man named Zerubbabel
Who had only one real, and one rubber ball.
When they asked if his pleasure
Was only half measure,
He replied, 'That is highly improbable.'
1941

A young man from Peloponnesus
Seduced all his nephews and nieces.
At the point of a sword
He married his ward.
And was the father of triplets, by Jesus.
1941

There was a young man named Morel
Who played with his prick till he fell,
When to get up he started
He suddenly farted,
And fell down again from the smell.
1943

If you're speaking of actions immoral
Then how about giving the laurel
To doughty Queen Esther,
No three men could best her,
One fore, one aft, and one oral.
1941

An opera singer named Black
Would f*** anything with a crack:
Sidewalks and board fences,
Young goats and cheese blintzes,
And the cheekiest man in his claque.
1945

A certain young lady named Daisy
Who is really infernally lazy
Said, 'I haven't the time
To wipe my behind,
But the way I can hump drives 'em crazy.'
1941

An ingenious young fellow named Herman
Tied a bow on the end of his worm, and
His wife said, 'How festive!'
But he said, 'Don't be restive,
You'll wiggle it off with your squirmin'.'
1941

A young lady sat by the sea,
Just as proper as proper could be.
A young fellow goosed her,
And roughly seduced her,
So she thanked him and went home to tea.
1941

There was a young girl of Bavaria
Who thought her disease was malaria.
But the family doc
Remarked to her shock,
'It is in the mercurial area.'
1941

A young baseball fan named Miss Glend
Was the home team's best rooter and friend,
But for her the big league
Never held the intrigue
Of a bat with two balls at the end.
1943

There was a young fellow from Lees
Who handled his tool with great ease.
This continual friction
Made his sex a mere fiction,
But the callus hangs down to his knees.
1947

A hoary old monk of Regina
Once said, 'There is nothing diviner
Than to sit in one's cell
And let one's mind dwell
On the charms of the Virgin's vagina.'
1941

There was a young lady of Bahore
Who was courted by gallants galore.
Their ardent protestin'
She found interestin',
And ended her life as a virgin.
1943

A lady with features cherubic
Was famed for her area pubic.
When they asked her its size
She replied in surprise,
'Are you speaking of square feet, or cubic?'
1941

There once was a yokel of Beaconsfield
Engaged to look after the deacon's field,
But he lurked in the ditches
And diddled the bitches
Who happened to cross that antique 'un's field.
1941

'My back aches. My penis is sore.
I simply can't f*** anymore.
I'm dripping with sweat,
And you haven't come yet;
And, my God! It's a quarter to four!'
1941

Harlot of Crete
Five verses

There was a young harlot of Crete
Whose f***ing was far, far too fleet.
So they tied down her ass
With a long ton of brass
To give them a much longer treat.

When the Nazis landed in Crete
The young harlot had to compete
With the many Storm Troopers
Who were using their poopers
For other things than to excrete.

Our subversive young harlot of Crete
Was led to fifth-column deceit.
When the paratroops landed
Her trade she expanded
By at once going down on their meat.

Then here was this harlot of Crete
She decided to be very neat.
She said, 'I'm too high class
To ream common ass,
And I'll wash every prick that I eat.'

And at last this young harlot of Crete
Was hawking her meat in the street.
Ambling out one fine day
In a casual way
She clapped up the whole British fleet.
1943

There was a young lady from Brussels
Who was proud of her vaginal muscles.
She could easily plex them
And so interflex them
As to whistle love songs through her bustles.
1941

A highly aesthetic young Jew
Had eyes of a heavenly blue;
The end of his dillie
Was shaped like a lily,
And his balls were too utterly two!
1941

A milkmaid there was, with a stutter,
Who was lonely and wanted a futter.
She had nowhere to turn,
So she diddled a churn,
And managed to come with the butter.
1941

A widow who lived in Rangoon
Hung a black-ribboned wreath on her womb,
'To remind me,' she said,
'Of my husband who's dead,
And of what put him into his tomb.'
1941

A once-famous gatherer of leeches
Has taken to combing the beaches,
Where he helps all his aunties
On and off with their panties,
And they help him off with his breeches.
1942

There was a young fellow named Gluck
Who found himself shit out of luck.
Though he petted and wooed,
When he tried to get screwed
He found virgins just don't give a f***.
1941

The Harlot's family
Four Verses

There was a young harlot named Schwartz
Whose cockpit was studded with warts,
And they tickled so nice
She drew a high price
From the studs at the summer resorts.

Her pimp, a young fellow named Biddle,
Was seldom hard up for a diddle,
For according to rumour
His tool had a tumour
And a fine row of warts down the middle.

Her brother, a bastard named Ben,
Could rotate his pecker, and then
He would shoot through his rear
Which made him the dear
Of the girls, and the envy of men.

Her other young brother, named Saul,
Was able to bounce either ball,
He could stretch them and snap them,
And juggle and clap them,
Which earned him the plaudits of all.
1941

A young man by a girl was desired
To give her the thrills she required,
But he died of old age
Ere his cock could assuage
The volcanic desire it inspired.
1941

There once was a tart named Belinda
Whose c*** opened out like a window.
But she'd slam the thing shut,
The contemptible slut,
Whenever you tried to get in her.
1941

Antoinette was a beautiful whore
Who wore fifty-six beads – nothing more.
They sneered, 'Unrefined!'
When she wore them behind,
So she tactfully wore them before.
1941

There was a young man of Cob Lenz
Whose ballocks were simply immense:
It took forty-four draymen,
A priest and three laymen
To carry them thither and hence.
1941

And then there's a story that's fraught
With disaster, of balls that got caught,
When a chap took a crap
In the woods, and a trap
Underneath . . . Oh, I can't bear the thought!
1941

A lazy, fat fellow named Betts
Upon his fat ass mostly sets.
Along comes a gal
And says, 'I'll f*** you, pal.'
Says he, 'If you'll do the work, let's.'
1941

There was a young man of Pitlochery
Whose morals were simply a mockery,
For under his bed
He'd a woman, instead
Of the usual item of crockery
1941

There was an old spinster of Tyre
Who bellowed, 'My c*** is on fire!'
So a fireman was found,
Brought his engine around,
And extinguished her burning desire.
1941

A promiscuous person named Willie
Had a dong that was simply a dilly.
He would take on all mammals
And was partial to camels,
But they never could tolerate Willie.
1942

There was a young lady named Ames
Who would play at the jolliest games.
She was great fun to lay
For her rectum would play
Obbligatos, and call you bad names.
1941

There was a young girl of Peru
Who had nothing whatever to do,
So she sat on the stairs
And counted her hairs,
Four thousand, three hundred, and two.
1941

There once was a newspaper vendor,
A person of dubious gender.
He would charge one-and-two
For permission to view
His remarkable double pudenda.
1941

There was an old whore of Azores
Whose c*** was all covered with sores.
The dogs in the street
Wouldn't eat the green meat
That hung in festoons from her drawers.
1941

The physicians of Countess von Krapp
Found a terrible rash on her map –
Sores that opened and closed
Which they soon diagnosed
As a case of perennial clap.
1941

A wide-bottomed girl named Trasket
Had a hole as big as a basket.
A spot, as a bride,
In it now, you could hide,
And include with your luggage your mascot.
1946

There was a young fellow from Parma
Who was solemnly screwing his charmer.
Said the damsel, demure,
'You'll excuse me, I'm sure,
But I must say you f*** like a farmer.'
1941

Have you heard of young Franchot Tone,
Who felt of his own peculiar bone?
It was long and quite narrow
And filled full of marrow,
And less edible than stale corn pone.
1941

There once was a sailor named Gasted,
A swell guy, as long as he lasted,
He could jerk himself off
In a basket, aloft,
Or a breeches-buoy swung from the masthead.
1941

There was a young virgin named Alice
Who thought of her c*** as a chalice.
One night, sleeping nude,
She awoke feeling lewd,
And found in her chalice a phallus.
1941

There was a young man from Thrisk,
Whose method of screwing was brisk.
And his reason was: 'If
The damned bitch has the syph,
This way I'm reducing the risk.'
1941

There was a young girl of Moline
Whose f***ing was sweet and obscene.
She would work on a prick
With every known trick,
And finish by winking it clean.
1941

There was an old man of Cajon
Who never could get a good bone.
With the aid of a gland
It grew simply grand;
Now his wife cannot leave it alone.
1941

There was a young fellow named Pell
Who didn't like c*** very well.
He would finger and f*** one,
But never would suck one,
He just couldn't get used to the smell.
1941

There was a young girl named McCall
Whose c*** was exceedingly small,
But the size of her anus
Was something quite heinous,
It could hold seven pricks and one ball.
1941

There was a young man who said, 'Why
Can't I bugger myself, if I'm spry?
If I put my mind to it
I'm sure I can do it,
You never can tell till you try.'
1941

A mathematician named Hall
Had a hexahedronical ball,
And the cube of its weight
Times his pecker, plus eight,
Was four-fifths of five-eighths of f***-all.
1941

There was a young girl named Louise
With a marvellous vaginal squeeze.
She inspired such pleasure
In her lover's yard measure,
That she caused his untimely decease.
1941

There was a young man of Arras
Who stretched himself out on the grass,
And with no little trouble
He bent himself double
And stuck his prick well up his ass.
1941

There was a young lady named May
Who strolled in the park by the way,
And she met a young man
Who f***ed her and ran,
Now she goes to the park everyday.
1941

An eccentric young poet named Brown
Raised up his embroidered gown
To look for his peter
To beat it to meter,
And fainted when none could be found.
1941

The prick of a young man of Kew
Showed veins that were azure of hue.
It's head was quite red
So he waved it and said,
'Three cheers for the red, white, and blue.'
1941

A pious young lady named Finnegan
Would caution her beau, 'Now you're in again,
Please watch it just right
So you'll last through the night,
For I certainly don't want to sin again.'
1941

There was a young girl of Pawtucket
Whose box was as big as a bucket.
Her boyfriend said, 'Toots,
I'll have to wear boots,
For I see I must muck it, not f*** it.'
1941

There was a young German named Ringer
Who was screwing an opera singer.
Said he with a grin,
'Well, I've sure got it in!'
Said she, 'You mean that ain't your finger?'
1941

There was a young lady named Ames
Who would play at the jolliest games.
She was great fun to lay
For her rectum would play
Obbligatos, and call you bad names.
1941

There was a young girl of Peru
Who had nothing whatever to do,
So she sat on the stairs
And counted c*** hairs,
Four thousand, three hundred, and two.
1941

Have you heard of young Franchot Tone
Who felt of his own peculiar bone?
It was long and quite narrow
And filled full of marrow,
And less edible than stale corn pone.
1941

A fellow with love-making flair
Was licking his sweetie 'down there.'
He said, as some gas
Escaped from her ass,
'Thank God for a breath of fresh air!'

All the lady-apes ran from King Kong
For his dong was unspeakably long.
But a friendly giraffe
Quaffed his yard and a half,
And ecstatically burst into song.
1941

An ignorant virgin of Dee
Entertained a man's cock just to see
If the damn thing would fit –
It went off in her pit,
And she said, 'Hey! That's no place to pee!'
1941

A young man maintained that his trigger
Was so big that there weren't any bigger.
But this long and thick pud
Was so heavy it could
Scarcely lift up its head. It lacked vigour.
1941

There was a young man of Savannah,
Met his end in a curious manner.
He diddled a hole
In a telegraph pole
And electrified his banana.
1941

There was a young lady whose thighs,
When spread showed a slit of such size,
And so deep and so wide,
You could play cards inside,
Much to her bridegroom's surprise.
1941

There were two Greek girls of Miletus
Who said, 'We wear gadgets that treat us,
When strapped on the thigh
Up cosy and high,
To constant, convenient coitus.'
1941

While f***ing one night, Dr Zuck
His wife's nipples in his ears stuck.
Then, his thumb up her bum,
He could hear himself come,
Thus inventing the Radio F***.
1941

Then on further experiment bent,
An improvement he thought he'd invent:
With his prick as conductor,
Combed her bush as he f***ed her,
And his balls shot off sparks when she spent.
1941

There was a young lady of Arden,
The tool of whose swain wouldn't harden.
Said she with a frown,
'I've been sadly let down
By the tool of a fool in a garden.'
1941

There was an old man of Duluth
Whose cock was shot off in his youth.
He f***ed with his nose
And with fingers and toes,
And he came through a hole in his tooth.
1941

Said a girl from Staraya Russia,
Whom the war had made looser and looser,
'Yes, I'm wormin' a German,
A vermin named Hermann,
But his dink is a lollapalooza!'
1942

There was a young fellow named Brewster
Who said to his wife as he goosed her,
'It used to be grand
But just look at my hand;
You ain't wiping as clean as you used to.'
1942

There was a young girl from Dakota
Had a letter from Ike: he wrote her:
'In addition to gas,
We're rationing ass,
And you've greatly exceeded your quota.'
1942

A grey-headed tutor named Polson
From some strange amatory contortion
Believed he'd conceived
A book, but relieved
Himself by a pamphlet abortion.
1942

There was a young fellow named Rule
Who went to a library school.
As he fingered the index
His thoughts ran to sex,
And his blood all ran to his tool.
1942

At the moment Japan declared war
A sailor was f***ing a whore.
He said, 'After this poke
'Long and hard' ain't no joke;
This means months till I get back ashore.'
1942

Have you heard of Professor MacKay
Who lays all the girls in the hay?
Though he thinks it's romantic
He drives them all frantic
By talking a wonderful lay.
1942

Quoth the coroner's jury in Preston,
'The verdict is rectal congestion.'
They found an eight-ball
On a shoemaker's awl
Halfway up the major's intestine.
1942

On May Day the girls of Penzance,
Being bored by the lack of romance,
Joined the workers' parade
With this banner displayed:
'What the Pants of Penzance Need is Ants.'
1941

Pity the spermatozoa!
His life leads him lower and lower.
With fear in his belly
He swims through the jelly,
But seldom increases the scoah.
1941

There was a young fellow named Rummy
Who delighted in whipping his dummy.
He played pocket pool
With his happy old tool
Till his shorts and his pants were all comey.
1942

A whorehouse at 9 Rue de Rennes
Had trouble in luring in men,
Till they got some fairies
With pretty dillberries,
And their clientele came back again.
1942

A lecherous fellow named Babbitt
Asked a girl if she'd f*** or would nab it.
Said she, 'From long habit
I f*** like a rabbit,
So I'd rather cohabit than grab it.'
1941

There was a young fellow named Babbitt
Who could screw nine times like a rabbit,
But a girl from Johore
Could do it twice more,
Which is just enough extra to crab it.
1942

Dame Catherine of Ashton-on-Lynches
Got on with her grooms and her wenches:
She went down on the gents,
And pronged the girls' vents
With a clitoris reaching six inches.
1942

Meat-rationing did not terrify Miss Davey,
She got married to a sailor in the Navy,
For she knew between his legs
He had ham and he had eggs,
A big weenie, and oodles of white gravy.
1942

There was an old maid in Van Nuys
Who went crazy from making mud pies.
She would fill them with farts
And pickled beef-hearts,
And bake them between her fierce thighs.
1942

There was an old sheik named Al Hassid
Whose tool had become very placid.
Before each injection
To get an erection
He had to immerse it in acid.
1949

There was a young man from Nargansett
Who coloured his prick to enhance it.
But the girls were afraid
That ere they got laid
'Twould lose all it's colour in transit.
1943

A star-gazing fellow named Flipper
Had a girl try to open his zipper.
As he stared at Orion,
The young girl was cryin'
As she found it was NOT a Big Dipper.
1942

There was a young girl named Dale
Who put up her ass for sale.
For the sum of two bits
You could tickle her tits,
But a buck would get you real tail.
1942

There was a young fellow named Malcolm
Who dusted his asshole with talcum.
He'd always use it
Everytime that he shit,
And found the sensation right welcome.
1942

There was a young nurse in Japan
Who lifts men by their pricks to the pan.
A trick of jujitsu,
And either it shits you
Or makes you feel more like a man.
1942

In Glasgow a tender tapeworm
Was so starved that he barely could squirm,
Until his host finally
Was buggered divinely,
And Jimmie had Vaseline and sperm.
1942

A sheep-herder in Van Buren
Lost half of his flock with the murrain.
Quoth the state veterinary,
'You ought not to carry
Them live spirochetes of your'n.'
1942

There was an old maid in Van Nuys
Who went crazy from making mud pies.
She would fill them with farts
And pickled beef-hearts,
And bake them between her fierce thighs.
1942

There was a young girl named Dale
Who put up her ass for sale.
For the sum of two bits
You could tickle her tits,
But a buck would get you real tail.
1942

There was a young fellow named Malcolm
Who dusted his ass-hole with talcum.
He'd always use it
Every time that he shit,
And found the sensation right welcome.
1942

A squeamish young fellow named Brand
Thought caressing his penis was grand,
But he viewed with distaste
The gelatinous paste
That it left in the palm of his hand.
1942

A virgin felt urged in Toulouse
Till she thought she would try self-abuse.
In search of a hard on
She ran out in the garden,
And was had by a statue of Zeus.
1942

There was a young lady named Mabel
Who liked to sprawl out on the table,
Then cry to her man,
'Stuff in all you can,
Get your ballocks in, too, if you're able.'
1943

There was a young lady named Riddle
Who had an untouchable middle.
She had many friends
Because of her ends,
Since it isn't the middle you diddle.
1943

A young polo player of Berkeley
Made love to his sweetheart berserkly.
In the midst of each chucker
He would break off and f*** her
Horizontally, laterally, and verkeley.
1943

There was a young artist named Victor
Who purchased a boa constrictor.
He intended to sketch her,
But decided (the lecher!)
To f*** her instead of depict her.
1943

There was a young fellow named Kelly
Who preferred his wife's ass to her belly.
He shrieked with delight
As he ploughed through the shite,
And filled up her hole with his jelly.
1942

An earnest young woman in Thrace
Said, 'Darling, that's not the right place!'
So he gave her a thwack,
And did on her back
What he couldn't have done face to face.
1942

Oden the bardling averred
His muse was the bum of a bird,
And his lesbian wife
Would finger his fife
While Fisherwood waited as third.
1942

There was a young lady named Astor
Who never let any get past her.
She finally got plenty
By stopping at twenty,
Which certainly ought to last her.
1942

When Abelard near Notre Dame
Had taught his fair pupil the game,
Her uncle, the wag
Cut off Peter's bag,
And his lectures were never the same.
1942

There was a young lady named Blunt
Who had a rectangular c***.
She learned for diversion
Posterior perversion
Since no one could fit her in front.
1943

A young bride was once heard to say,
'Oh dear, I am wearing away!
The insides of my thighs
Look just like mince pies,
For my husband won't shave every day.'
1943

Any whore whose door sports a red light
Knows a prick when she sees one, all right.
She can tell by a glance
At the drape of men's pants
If they're worth taking on for the night.
1943

There was an old soldier named Schmitt
Took a trip to the can for to shit.
To his epic despair
No paper was there.
So he simply continued to sit.
1943

There once was a girl from the chorus
Whose virtue was known to be porous.
She started by candling,
And ended by handling
The whole clientele of a whorehouse.
1943

There was a stout lady of Cuttack
Posteriorly pecked by a wild duck
Who pursued her for miles
And continued his wiles
Till he completely demolished her buttock.
1943

There was a young man from New Haven
Who had an affair with a raven.
He said with a grin
As he wiped off his chin,
'Nevermore!'
1943

An amorous Jew, on Yom Kippur,
Saw a shiksel and decided to clip her.
'I'll grip her, and strip her,
And lip her, and whip her,'
Then his dingus shot off in his zipper!
1943

There was a young man from Narragansett
Who coloured his prick to enhance it.
But the girls were afraid
That ere they got laid
'Twould lose all it's colour in transit.
1943

An ardent young man from Narragansett
Was accustomed to f***ing in transit.
He'd catch something neat
In a Pullman retreat,
Say 'How do you do?', and then pants it.
1945

There was a young damsel named Baker
Who was poked in a pew by a Quaker.
He yelled, 'My God! what
Do you call this, a twat?
Why, the entrance is more than an acre!'
1943

A lazy young lady named May
Was a torrid but troublesome lay,
She was prone to conceive,
So made haste to achieve
A bed with a built-in bidet.
1943

There was a young lady of Spain
Who was f***ed by a monk in a drain.
They did it again,
And again and again,
And again and again and again.
1943

There was a young man named Morel
Who played with his prick till he fell,
When to get up he started
He suddenly farted,
And fell down again from the smell.
1943

There was a young man, name of Snyder,
Who took out a girl just to ride her.
She allowed him to feel
From her neck to her heel,
But never would let him inside her.
1943

There was a young fellow named Harry,
Had a joint that was long, huge and scary.
He pressed it on a virgin
Who, without any urgin',
Immediately spread like a fairy.
1943

A morbid young lady named Jean
Was known as the Masochist Queen.
She used thistles and cacti
In pursuit of her practi,
In a manner both odd and obscene.
1943

There once was a fellow named Siegel
Who attempted to bugger a beagle,
But the mettlesome bitch
Turned and said with a twitch,
'It's fun, but you know it's illegal.'
1943

A decayed, witty old frump of Thrace
Substituted rubber in her personal place.
She developed the trick,
When you pulled out your prick,
Of snapping the guck in your face.
1943

There was a young lady named Grace
Who took all she could in her face,
But an adequate lad
Gave her all that he had,
And blew tonsils all over the place.
1943

A virile young GI named Shorty
Was lively, and known to be 'sporty.'
But he once made a slip
And showed up with a 'drip,'
And was red-lined (35-1440).
1943

There was a debauched little wench
Whom nothing could ever make blench.
She admitted men's poles
At all possible holes,
And she'd bugger, f***, jerk off, and French.
1943

A Salvation Lassie named Claire
Was having her first love affair.
As she climbed into bed
She reverently said,
'I wish to be opened with prayer.'
1943

There was a young lady named Inge
Who went on a binge with a dinge.
Now I won't breathe a word
Of what really occurred,
But her c*** has a chocolate fringe.
1943

An old G.I. custom long-rooted
Is to entering fledglings well-suited.
In every latrine
A bright sign is seen:
'Stand close, the next guy may be barefooted.'
1943

There was a young fellow named Fletcher,
Was reputed an infamous lecher.
When he'd take on a whore
She'd need a rebore,
And they'd carry him out on a stretcher.
1943

There was a young man of Baghdad
Who was dreaming that he was a shad.
He dreamt he was spawning,
And then, the next morning,
He found that, by Jesus!, he had.
1944

The sex of the asteroid vermin
Is exceedingly hard to determine.
The galactic patrol
Simply f***s any hole
That will possibly let all the sperm in.
1944

There was a young fellow named Spratt
Who was terribly sassy and fat.
He sat amusing himself
By abusing himself,
While his trained leopard licked at his pratt.
1944

There once was a Bishop of Treet
Who decided to be indiscreet,
But after one round
To his horror he found
You repeat, and repeat, and repeat.
1944

There was a long lady named Weaver
Who had intercourse with a beaver.
The result of their f***
Was a canvas-back duck,
Two muskrats and a hump-backed retriever.

There was a young blade from South Greece
Whose bush did so greatly increase
That before he could shack
He must hunt needle in stack,
'Twas as bad as his being obese.
1944

There was a young squaw of Wohunt
Who possessed a collapsible c***.
It had many odd uses,
Produced no papooses,
And fitted both giant and runt.
1944

My wife Myrtle's womb has a habit
Of expanding whenever I stab it.
What's more, my wife Myrtle
Is so wondrously fertile,
That she's giving me kids like a rabbit.
1944

There was a young fellow named Jim
Whose wife kept a worm in her quim.
It was silly and smelly
And tickled her belly,
And what the hell was it to him?
1944

Said a certain sweet red-headed siren,
'Young sailors are cute, I must try one!'
She came home in the nude,
Stewed, screwed, and tattooed
With lewd pictures and verses from Byron.
1944

A worried young man from Istanbul
Discovered red spots on his tool.
Said the doctor, a cynic,
'Get out of my clinic!
Just wipe off the lipstick, you fool!'
1944

I once was annoyed by a queer
Who made his intentions quite clear.
Said I, 'I'm no prude,
So don't think me rude,
But I'm already stewed, screwed, and tattooed.'
1944

On the plains of north-central Tibet
They've thought of the strangest thing yet:
On the ass of a camel
They pour blue enamel,
And bugger the beast while it's wet.
1944

A disgusting young man named McGill
Made his neighbours exceedingly ill
When they learned of his habits
Involving white rabbits
And a bird with a flexible bill.
1944

The notorious Duchess of Peels
Saw a fisherman fishing for eels.
Said she, 'Would you mind?
Shove one up my behind.
I am anxious to know how it feels.'
1944

There was a young girl named Dalrymple
Whose sexual needs were so simple.
She enjoyed the full spasm
Of a perfect orgasm
By frigging herself on a pimple.
1944

There was an old fellow named Rapp
Who had a job all considered a snap.
In the insane asylum
He'd grade c***s and file 'em,
And bi-weekly he'd rub up their nap.
1944

A very odd pair are the Pitts:
His balls are as large as her tits,
Her tits are as large
As an invasion barge,
Neither knows how the other cohabits.
1944

There was a young girl from Eau Claire
Who once was attacked by a bear.
While chased in a field
She tripped and revealed
Some meat to the bear that was rare.
1944

There was a young sailor named Bates
Who did the fandango on skates.
He fell on his cutlass
Which rendered him nutless
And practically useless on dates.
1944

There was an asexual bigot
Whose cock only served as a spigot,
Till a jolly young whore
Taught him tricks by the score
Now his greatest delight is to frig it.
1944

A team of Tom and Louise
Do an act in the nude on their knees.
They crawl down the aisle
While f***ing dog-style,
And the orchestra plays Kolmer's '*Trees*'.
1945

A lecherous Northumbrian druid,
Whose mind was filthy and lewd,
Awoke from a trance
With his hand in his pants
On a lump of pre-seminal fluid.
1945

There was a young fellow of Warwick
Who had reason for feeling euphoric,
For he could by election
Have triune erection:
Ionic, Corinthian, Doric.
1945

There once was a dentist named Stone
Who saw all his patients alone.
In a fit of depravity
He filled the wrong cavity,
And my, how his practice has grown!
1945

A glutted debauchee from Frome
Lured beauteous maids to his room,
Where, after he'd strip 'em,
He'd generally whip 'em
With a bundle of twigs or a broom.
1945

The dong of a fellow named Grable
Was as pliant and long as a cable.
Each night while he ate,
This confirmed reprobate
Would screw his wife under the table.
1945

An ardent young man from Narragansett
Was accustomed to f***ing in transit.
He'd catch something neat
In a Pullman retreat,
Say 'How do you do?,' and then pants it.
1945

There was a young fellow named Meek
Who invented a lingual technique,
It drove women frantic
And made them romantic,
And wore all the hair off his cheek.
1945

There was a young lady named Rackstraw,
Titillated herself with a hack-saw.
As a result of this action
She no longer has traction,
And a penis feels just like a jackstraw.
1945

A progressive and young Eskimo
Grew tired of his squaw, and so
Slipped out of his hut
To look for a slut
Who knew the very fine art of Blow.
1946

A sultan named Abou ben Adhem
Thus cautioned a travelling madam,
'I suffer from crabs
As do most us A-rabs,'
'It's alright,' said the madam, 'I've had 'em.'
1946

A depraved old Jew from Estretto
Buggered every young man in the ghetto.
He once had his hose in
A musician, composing,
Who said: 'Not so slow, allegretto!'
1946

There was a young man from Wanamee
Well schooled in the technique of sodomy.
He buggered with glee
An old man in a tree,
And remarked with a shrug, 'Won't you pardon me?'
1946

A fair-haired young damsel named Grace
Thought it very, very foolish to place
Her hand on your cock
When it turned hard as rock,
For fear it would explode in her face.
1946

There is a young faggot named Mose
Who insists that you f*** his long nose.
And you'll double the joy
Of this lecherous boy
If you'll tickle his balls with your toes.
1946

Peter, first Duke of Orange
Was limited to a miserable four-inch,
But technique in a keyhole
Developed his P-hole
Til at last it got caught in the door-hinge.
1946

A Self-Centred Young Fellow Named Newcombe

A self-centred young fellow named Newcombe
Who seduced many girls but made few come
Said, 'The pleasures of tail
Were ordained for the male.
I've had mine. Do I care whether you come?'

She egged him on with her charms,
And wriggled right into his arms.
She promised him bliss
With her first little kiss,
And they soon found themselves in a barn.

She slid under his much-muscled torso
And guided his shaft to her morceau.
He drilled till she ran
Ane dripped into a pan,
She was filled like she'd wished, only more so.
1946

There was a young man from Bengal
Who got in a hole in a wall.
'Oh,' he said, 'It's a pity
This hole is so gritty,
But it's better than nothing at all.'
1946

Ethnologists up with the Sioux
Wired home for two punts, one canoe.
The answer next day
Said, 'Girls on the way,
But what the hell's a "panoe"?'
1946

The king named Oedipus Rex
Who started this fuss about sex
Put the world to great pains
By the spots and the stains
Which he made on his mother's pubex.
1946

'I'll do it for Art, I'm no prude!'
He said, as he posed in the nude.
But on viewing his ass
The whole fairy class
Decided it ought to be screwed.
1946

A girl named Alice, in Dallas,
Had never felt of a phallus.
She remained virgo intacto,
Because, ipso facto,
No phallus in Dallas fit Alice.
1946

An Indian squaw up at Spruce
Was unable to have a papoose.
She said to her pater,
When he asked, 'What's the matter?'
'I can't swallow the foul, slimy juice.'
1946

A whimsical Arab from Aden
His masculine member well laden,
Cried: 'Nuptial joy,
When shared with a boy,
Is better than melon or maiden!'
1946

There was a young bounder named Link
Who possessed a very tart dink.
To sweeten it some
He steeped it in rum,
And he's driven the ladies to drink.
1946

There was a young lady named Kerr
Whose step-ins were made out of fur.
When they asked, 'Is it fun?'
She replied, 'It's a son-
Of-a-gun to make pussy purr!'
1946

There was a young man from the coast
Who received a parcel by post.
It contained, so I heard,
A triangular turd
And the balls of his grandfather's ghost.
1946

It always delights me at Hanks
To walk up the old river banks.
One time in the grass
I stepped on an ass,
And heard a young girl murmur, 'Thanks.'
1946

There's a pretty young lady named Sark,
Afraid to get laid in the dark,
But she's often manhandled
By the light of a candle
In the bushes of Gramercy Park.
1946

An explorer whose habits were blunt
Once flavoured some cannibal c***.
The asshole was shitty,
And, more was the pity,
It oozed from the rear to the front.
1946

There was a young man from Darjeeling
Whose dong reached up to the ceiling.
In the electric light socket
He'd put it and rock it,
Oh God! What a wonderful feeling!
1946

There was a young man named McNamiter
With a tool of prodigious diameter.
But it wasn't the size
Gave the girls a surprise,
But his rhythm, iambic pentameter.
1946

A eunuch who came from Port Said
Had a jolly good time in bed,
Nor could any sultana
Detect from his manner
That he used a banana instead.
1947

There was a young fellow named Veach
Who fell fast asleep on the beach.
His dreams of nude women
Had his proud organ brimmin'
And squirting on all within reach.
1947

I once had the wife of a Dean
Seven times while the Dean was out ski'in'.
She remarked with some gaiety,
'Not bad for the laity,
Though the Bishop once managed thirteen.'
1947

There was a young man from Racine
Who was weaned at the age of eighteen.
He said, 'I'll admit
There's no milk in the tit,
But think of the fun it has been.'
1947

There was a young girl of Alsace
Who was having her first piece of ass.
'Oh, Darling , you'll kill me!
Oh, Dearest, you thrill me
Like Father John's thumb after mass!'
1947

There was a young girl named O'Clare
Whose body was covered with hair.
It was really quite fun
To probe with one's gun,
For her quimmy might be anywhere.
1947

There was a young girl named Miss Randall
Who thought it beneath her to handle
A young fellow's pole,
So instead, her hot hole
She contented by means of a candle.
1947

There was a young man from Tahiti
Who went for a swim with his sweetie,
And as he pursued her
A blind barracuda
Ran off with his masculinity.
1947

There was a young man from Siam
Who said, 'I go in with a wham,
But I soon lose my starch
Like the mad month of March,
And the lion comes out like a lamb.'
1947

There is a young fellow from Leeds
Whose skin is so thin his cock bleeds
Whenever erect,
This dermal defect
Often scares him from sowing his seeds.
1947

In his garden remarked Lord Dunedin,
'A fig for your diggin' and weedin'.
I like watching birds
While they're dropping their turds,
And spyin' on guineapigs breedin''.
1947

There was a young fellow named Grimes
Who f***ed a girl seventeen times
In the course of a week,
And this isn't to speak
Of assorted venereal crimes.
1947

The monogamous man from Fyffe
Two verses

There was a young fellow named Fyffe
Whose marriage was ruined for life,
For he had an aversion
To every perversion,
And only liked f***ing his wife.

Well, one year the poor woman struck,
And she wept, and she cursed at her luck,
And said, 'Where have you gotten us
With your goddamn monotonous
F*** after f*** after f***?'
1947

There was a young girl of Antietam
Who liked horse turds so well she could eat 'em.
She'd lie on their rumps
And swallow the lumps
As fast as the beasts could excrete 'em.
1947

For sculpture that's really first class
You need form, composition, and mass.
To do a good Venus
Just leave off the penis,
And concentrate all on the ass.
1947

Have you heard of knock-kneed Samuel McGuzzun
Who married Samantha, his bow-legged cousin?
Some people say
Love finds a way,
But for Sam and Samantha, it doesn'.
1947

I dined with Lord Hughing Fitz-Bluing
Who said, 'Do you squirm when you're screwing?'
I replied, 'Simple shagging
Without any wagging
Is only for screwing canoeing.'
1947

There was a young man of Klutki
Who could blink himself off with one eye.
For a while though, he pined,
When his organ declined
To function, because of a stye.
1947

There once was a man named Enus
Who had a 50 foot penis.
It dragged on the ground,
And made a bad sound,
And when stiff it reached up to Venus.

Here's to old King Montezuma,
For fun he would bugger a puma.
The puma in play
Clawed both balls away,
How's that for animal humour?
1948

A lady who lived in Astoria
Took a fancy to Fletcher's Castoria.
She partook of this drink
With her ass in the sink,
Now I ask you: ain't that foresight for ya?
1948

A young man with a passion quite vast
Used to talk about making it last,
Till one day he discovered
His sister uncovered,
And now he f***s often, and fast.
1948

A rich old man named Ray
Who felt himself slipping away.
He endowed a large ward
In a house where he'd whored.
Was there a crowd at his funeral? I'll say!
1948

The prior of Dunstan St Just,
Consumed with erotic lust,
Raped the bishop's prize fowls,
Buggered four startled owls
And a little green lizard that bust.
1948

A girl with a sebaceous cyst
Always came when her asshole was kissed.
Her lover was gratified
That she was so satisfied,
But regretted the fun that he missed.
1948

Sue made a thing of soft leather,
And topped off the end with a feather.
When she poked it inside her,
She took off like a glider,
And gave up her lover forever.
1948

I'd rather have fingers than toes,
I'd rather have ears than a nose,
And a happy erection
Brought just to perfection
Makes me terribly sad when it goes.
1948

A vigorous fellow named Bert
Was attracted by every new skirt.
Oh, it wasn't their minds
But their rounded behinds
That excited this lovable flirt.
1948

There was a young girl of Des Moines
Whose c*** could be fitted with coins,
Till a guy from Hoboken
Went and dropped in a token,
And now she rides free on the ferry.
1948

On his honeymoon sailing the ocean
A tightwad displayed much emotion
When he learned, one fine day,
He'd been f***ing away
What could have been bottled as lotion.
1948

There once was a Monarch of Spain
Who was terribly haughty and vain.
When women were nigh
He'd unbutton his fly,
And screw them with signs of disdain.
1949

A versatile lady of Zaandam
Made appointments completely at random,
Since if two dates got mixed
It was easily fixed
By letting them screw her in tandem.
1949

There was a young fellow called Tom
Who ran screaming home to his mom.
The fear of the Bomb
Scared him back in the womb,
The bastard, he wasn't so dumb!
1950

There was a young man from Axminister
Whose designs were quite base and quite sinister.
His lifelong ambition
Was anal coition
With the wife of the French foreign minister.
1950

There was an old satyr named Mack
Whose prick had a left-handed tack.
If the ladies he loves
Don't spin when he shoves,
Their cervixes frequently crack.
1950

There was a young man named Murray
Who made love to a girl in a surrey.
She started to sigh
But someone walked by,
So he buttoned his pants in a hurry.
1950

There was a young person of Kent
Who was famous wherever he went.
All the way through a f***
He would quack like a duck,
And he crowed like a cock when he spent.
1951

To the mountains went sweet Dolly Dare
Intent upon having an affair,
But her plans they miscarried,
The guys were all married,
But you can bet she played no solitaire.
1951

There was an old maid from Bruton
Who had the bad habit of pootin'.
Her sphincter was weak,
Her wind she couldn't keep,
This tootin' old spinster from Bruton.
1951

There once was a lady named Hix
Who was fond of sucking big pricks.
One fellow she took
Was a doctor named Snook,
Now he's in a hell of a fix.
1952

There was a shy boy named Dan
Who tickled his girl with a fan.
She started to flirt
So he lifted her skirt
And gave her a f*** like a man.
1950

There once was a laddie of Neep
Who demanded everything cheap.
When he wanted to screw
There was nothing to do
But take out his passion on sheep.
1951

There was an eccentric from Mecca
Who discovered a record from Decca,
Which he twirled on his thumb
(These eccentrics are dumb)
While he needled the disc with his pecca.
1951

There was a young fellow named Tucker
Who rushed at his mother to f*** her.
His mother said, 'Damn!
Don't you know who I am?
You act like a regular mucker!'
1952

'It's dull in Duluth, Minnesota,
Of spirit, there's not an iota,'
Complained Alice to Joe,
Who tried not to show
That he yawned in her snatch as he blowed her.
1952

Said a Palestine pilgrim named Wadham,
'For religion I don't give a Goddem!
I've frequently peed in
The Garden of Eden,
And buggered my guide when in Sodom.'
1952

There was a young fellow named Runyan
Whose pecker came down with a bunion.
When he had an erection
This painful infection
Gave off a faint odour of onion.
1952

There was a young girl of Connecticut
Who didn't care much about etiquette.
Whenever she was able
She'd piss on the table,
And mop off her c*** with her petticoat.
1952

There was a young man from Saskatchewan
Whose pecker was truly gargantuan.
It was good for large whores,
And small dinosaurs,
And sufficiently rough to scratch a match upon.
1952

There was a young man of Province
Whose bollocks were simply immense.
'They're an excellent float
In a bathtub or boat,
But,' said he, 'what a bore when I yentz.'
1952

Said a lesbian lady, 'It's sad;
Of all of the girls that I've had,
None gave me the thrill
Of real rapture until
I learned how to be a tribade.'
1952

The skater, Barbara Ann Scott
Is so wonderfully 'winsome' a snot,
That when posed on her toes
She elaborately shows
Teeth, fat ass, titties, and twat.
1952

A scandal involving an oyster
Sent the Countess of Clews to a cloister.
She preferred it in bed
To the Count, so she said,
Being longer, and stronger, and moister.
1952

There's a dowager near Sweden's Landing
Whose manners are odd and demanding.
It's one of her jests
To suck off her guests,
She hates to keep gentlemen standing.
1952

A school marm from old Mississippi
Had a quim that was simply zippy.
The scholars all praised it
Till finally she raised it
To prices befitting a chippy.
1952

There lived in French Louisiana
A quaint and deceived old duenna
Who naively thought
That a penis was wrought
To be ate like a thick ripe banana.
1952

An aesthete from South Carolina
Had a cock that tinkled like china,
But while shooting his load
It cracked like old Spode,
So he's bought him a Steuben vagina.
1952

A rapturous young fellatrix
One day was at work on five pricks.
With an unholy cry
She whipped out her glass eye:
'Tell the boys I can now take on six.'
1952

There was a young lady named Shriver
Who was screwed in the ass by the driver,
And when she complained
He said, 'Sorry you were pained,'
And gave her a fiver to bribe her.
1952

Don't dip your wick in a Wac,
Don't ride the breast of a Wave,
Just sit in the sand
And do it by hand,
And buy bonds with the money you save.
1948

There was a young lady from Sydney
Who could take it right up to her kidney.
But a man from Quebec
Shoved it up to her neck.
He had a long one, now didn' he?
1943

There was a young lady from Teal
Who was raped in the lake by an eel.
One morning at dawn,
She gave birth to a prawn,
Two crabs, and a small baby seal.
1939

There's a charming young girl in Tobruk
Who refers to her quiff as a nook.
It's deep and it's wide,
You can curl up inside
With a nice easy chair and a book.
1946

There was a young lady of Samoa
Who plugged up her c*** with a boa.
This strange contraceptive
Was very deceptive
To all but the spermatozoa.
1941

There was a young lady named Moore
Who, while not quite precisely a whore,
Couldn't pass up a chance
To take down her pants,
And compare some man's stroke with her bore.
1941

There was an old Count of Swoboda
Who would not pay a whore what he owed her.
So with great savoir-faire
She stood on a chair,
And pissed in his whiskey and soda.
1938

A thrifty old man named McEwen
Inquired, 'Why be bothered with screwin?'
It's safer and cleaner
To finger your wiener,
And besides, you can see what you're doin'.'
1942

There was a young lady of Dover
Whose passion was such that it drove her
To cry, when she came,
'Oh dear! What a shame!
Well, now we shall have to start over.'
1941

A lady of virginal humours
Would only be screwed through her bloomers.
But one fatal day
The bloomers gave way,
Which fixed her for future consumers.
1941

The cock of a fellow named Randall
Shot sparks like a big Roman candle.
He was much in demand,
For the colours were grand,
But the girls found him too hot to handle.
1946

There was a young Nubian prince
Whose cock would make elephants wince.
Once, while socking the sperm
To a large pachyderm,
He slipped, and has not been seen since.
1943

There was a young Jewess named Hanna
Who sucked off her lover's banana.
She swore that the cream
That shot out in a stream
Tasted better than biblical Manna.
1942

There once was a girl named Louise
Whose c***-hair hung down to her knees.
The crabs in her twat
Tied the hair in a knot,
And constructed a flying trapeze.
1944

There was a young fellow named Bill
Who took an atomic pill.
His navel corroded,
His asshole exploded,
And they found both his nuts in Brazil.
1948

There once was a man of Cape Nod
Who attempted to bugger a cod,
When up came some scallops
And nibbled his bollops,
And now he's a eunuch, by God.
1930

A maestro directing in Rome
Had a quaint way of driving it home.
Whoever he climbed
Had to keep her tail timed
To the beat of his old metronome.
1942

There was a young man of high station
Who was found by a pious relation
Making love in a ditch
To – I won't say a bitch –
But a woman of no reputation.
1938

An agreeable girl named Miss Doves
Likes to jack off the young men she loves.
She will use her bare fist
If the fellows insist
But she really prefers to wear gloves.
1942

An old doctor who lacked protoplasm
Tried to give his young wife an orgasm,
But his tongue jumped the track
'Twixt the front and the back,
And got pinched in a bad anal spasm.
1947

There was a young man named Hughes
Who swore off all kinds of booze.
He said, 'When I'm muddled
My senses get fuddled,
And I pass up too many screws.'
1948

There was a young girl of Mobile
Whose hymen was made of chilled steel.
To give her a thrill,
Took a rotary drill
Or a Number 9 emery wheel.
1938

A detective named Ellery Queen
Has olfactory powers so keen,
He can tell in a flash
By the scent of a gash
Who its previous tenant has been.
1945

There was a young lady named Duff
With a lovely, luxuriant muff
In his haste to get in her
One eager beginner
Lost both his balls in the rough.
1941

There was a young fellow named Kimble
Whose prick was exceedingly nimble,
But fragile and slender,
And dainty and tender,
So he kept it encased in a thimble.
1941

A remarkable race are the Persians,
They have such peculiar diversions.
They screw the whole day
In the regular way,
And save up the nights for perversions.
1941

There once was a floozie named Annie
Whose prices were cosy, but canny:
A buck for a f***,
Fifty cents for a suck,
And a dime for a feel of her fanny.
1943

There was a young lady named Mandel
Who caused quite a neighbourhood scandal
By coming out bare
On the main village square
And frigging herself with a candle.
1943

A pious old woman named Tweak
Had taught her vagina to speak.
It was frequently liable
To quote from the Bible,
But when f***ing – not even a squeak.
1941

King Louis gave a lesson in class,
One time he was sexing a lass.
When she used the word, 'Damn,'
He rebuked her: 'Please ma'am,
Keep a more civil tongue in my ass.'
1950

There was a young man in the choir
Whose penis rose higher and higher,
Till it reached such a height
It was quite out of sight –
But of course you know I am a liar.
1946

A neuropath-virgin named Flynn
Shouted before she gave in:
'It isn't the deed,
Or the fear of the seed,
But that big worm that's shedding its skin!'
1942

Thus spake an old Chinese Mandarin,
'There's a subject I'd like to use candour in:
The geese of Pekin
Are so steeped in sin
They'd as soon let a man as a gander in.'
1941

There was a young fellow of Ealing,
Devoid of all delicate feeling.
When he read on the door:
'Don't shit on the floor'
He jumped up and shat on the ceiling.
1941

A young man, quite free with his dong,
Said the thing could be had for a song.
Such response did he get
That he rented the Met,
And held auditions all the day long.
1942

A charming young lady named Randall
Has a clap that the doctors can't handle.
So this lovely, lorn floozie,
With her poor, damaged coosie,
Must take her delight with a candle.
1941

A handsome young monk in a wood
Told a girl she should cling to the good.
She obeyed him, and gladly;
He repulsed her, but sadly:
'My dear, you have misunderstood.'
1943

There was a young lady named Myrtle
Whose womb was exceedingly fertile.
Her pa made contortions
At all her abortions,
And bought her a chastity girdle.
1944

There was a young trucker named Briard
Who had a young whore that he hired
To f*** when not trucking,
But trucking plus f***ing
Got him so f***ing tired he got fired.
1941

There was a young lady named Alice
Who peed in a Catholic chalice.
She said, 'I do this,
From a great need to piss,
And not from sectarian malice.'
1941

A Newfoundland lad from Placentia
Was in love to the point of dementia,
But his love couldn't burgeon
With his touch-me-not virgin
'Til he screwed her by hand in absentia.
1947

There was a young bride, a Canuck,
Told her husband, 'Let's do more than suck.
You say that I, maybe,
Can have my first baby –
Let's give up this Frenching, and f***!'
1943

There was a young girl of Llewellyn
Whose breasts were as big as a melon.
They were big, it is true,
But her c*** was big, too,
Like a bifocal, full-colour, aerial view
Of Cape Horn and the Straits of Magellan.
1941

There once was a son-of-a-bitch,
Neither clever, nor handsome, nor rich,
Yet the girls he would dazzle,
And f*** to a frazzle,
And then ditch them, the son-of-a-bitch.
1941

A young queer who was much oversexed
Was easily fretted and vexed.
When out on a date
He hardly could wait
To say, 'Turn over, bud; my turn next.'
1942

There was a young lady who said,
As her bridegroom got into the bed,
'I'm tired of this stunt
That they do with one's c***,
You can get up my bottom instead.'
1951

The latest reports from Good Hope
State that apes there have pricks thick as rope,
And f*** high, wide, and free,
From the top of one tree
To the top of the next. What a scope!
1941

There once was a passionate Celt
Who'd an urge to know how a cock felt.
One went in hard and straight
But her heat was so great
That she found she had caused it to melt.
1941

A habit obscene and bizarre
Has taken a-hold of papa:
He brings home young camels
And other odd mammals,
And gives them a go at mama.
1946

'The testes are cooler outside,'
Said the doc to the curious bride,
'For the semen must not
Get too f***ing hot,
And the bag fans your bum on the ride.'
1942

There was a young man, a Maltese,
Who could even screw horses with ease.
He'd flout natural laws
In this manner because
Of his dong, which hung down to his knees.
1943

There was young lady from 'Quoddie
Who had a magnificent body,
And her face was not bad,
Yet she'd never been had
For her odour was markedly coddy.
1949

There once was a lady who'd sinned,
Who said as her abdomen thinned,
'By my unsullied honour,
I'm not a madonna!
My baby has gone with the wind.'
1947

A newlywed man in Peru
Found himself in a terrible stew:
His wife was in bed
Much deader than dead,
And so he had no one to screw.
1946

Young girls of seductive proportions
Should take contraceptive precautions:
Silly young Ermintrude
Let one small sperm intrude . . .
Who's the best man for abortions?
1958

In the pitch black dark of the mill
An old man made history still.
Said he, with Viagra,
When he bent down to grab ya,
'Don't worry babe, I'm on the pill.

There was a young girl named Dinwiddie
With a brace of voluptuous titty.
But the boys squeezed them so
That they hung down below,
And one drooped behind and got shitty.
1941

There was an old lady of Ypres
Who got shot in the ass by some snipers,
And when she blew air
Through the holes that were there,
She astonished the Cameron Pipers.
1941

A lusty young woodsman of Maine
For years with no woman had lain,
But he found sublimation
At a high elevation
In the crotch of a pine. God, the pain!
1941

A stout Gaelic warrior, McPherson,
Was having a captive, a person
Who was not averse
Though she had the curse,
And he'd breeches of bristling furs on.
1942

There once was a sergeant named Schmitt
Who wanted a crime to commit.
He thought raping women
Was a little too common,
So he buggered an aged tomtit.
1944

There once was a brilliant young poet
Who loved it – wouldn't you know it?
When you'd want to six nine
His penis would pine.
'I just can't,' it said; 'I can't go it.'
1942

There once was a man named O'Malley
Who was frigging a lassie named Sally.
The first words she spoke,
As he gave her a poke,
Were 'Mister, you're right up my alley'.

There was a young man of Tibet,
And this is the strangest one yet.
His prick was so long,
And so pointed and strong,
He could bugger six Greeks en brochette.
1941

There was a young lady of Rhodes
Who sinned in unusual modes.
At the height of her fame
She abruptly became
The mother of four dozen toads.
1943

There was an old man of Tagore
Whose tool was a yard long or more,
So he wore the damn thing
In a surgical sling
To keep it from wiping the floor.
1941

There was a young lady named Nelly
Whose tits could be joggled like jelly.
They could tickle her twat,
Or be tied in a knot,
And could even swat flies on her belly.
1941

A young curate, just new to the cloth,
At sex was surely no sloth.
He preached masturbation
To his whole congregation,
And was washed down the aisle in the froth.
1946

The wife of a chronic crusader
Took on every man who waylaid her.
Till the amorous itch
Of this popular bitch
So annoyed the crusader he spayed her.
1942

There was a young man of Madras
Whose balls were constructed of brass.
When jangled together
They played 'Stormy Weather,'
And lightning shot out of his ass.
1938

There was a young fellow of Kent
Who had a peculiar bent.
He collected the turds
Of various birds,
And had them for lunch during Lent.
1947

There once was a jolly old bloke
Who picked up a girl for a poke.
He took down her pants,
F***ed her into a trance,
And then shit in her shoe for a joke.
1941

A lisping young lady named Beth
Was saved from a fate worse than death
Seven times in a row,
Which unsettled her so
That she quit saying 'No' and said 'Yeth.'
1941

An old couple just at Shrovetide
Were having a piece – when he died.
The wife for a week
Sat tight on his peak,
And bounced up and down as she cried.
1942

A lady athletic and handsome
Got wedged in her sleeping room transom.
When she offered much gold
For release, she was told
That the view was worth more than the ransom.
1944

There was a young girl named Heather
Whose twitcher was made out of leather.
She made a queer noise,
Which attracted the boys,
By flapping the edges together.
1945

There once was a pretty young miss
Who enjoyed watching her lover piss.
She made him drink water
Much more than he oughter,
While pilsner assured her of bliss.
1942

A chappie whose name was O'Dare
Sailed on a ship to Kenmare,
But this cute little honey
Had left home her money
So she laid the whole crew for her fare.
1946

There was a young lady of Totten
Whose tastes grew perverted and rotten.
She cared not for steaks,
Or for pastry and cakes,
But lived upon penis au gratin.
1938

A man who is lacking in pride
Attends funerals far, near, and wide.
When asked about this
His reply is, ''Tis bliss
To bugger a piece of dead hide.'
1946

'Far dearer to me than my treasure,'
The Heiress declared, 'is my leisure.
For then I can screw
The whole Harvard crew,
They're slow, and that lengthens the pleasure.'
1941

A horny young girl of Madras
Reclined with a monk on the grass.
She tickled his cock
With the end of a rock
Till it foamed like a bottle of Bass.
1941

There was a young girl of Des Moines
Who had a large sack full of coins.
The nickels and dimes
She got from the times
That she cradled the boys in her loins.
1945

A big Catholic Layman named Fox
Makes his living by sucking off cocks.
In spells of depression
He goes to confession
And jacks off the priest in his box.
1945

The modern cinematic emporium
Is by no means the merest sexorium,
But a highly effectual
Heterosexual
Mutual masturbatorium.
1943

There once was a sacred baboon
That lived by the river Rangoon,
And all of the women
That came to go swimmin'
He'd bang by the light of the moon.
1941

A perverted old barber once said,
'I never can trim a man's head,
'Cause I wish that his jowls
Were nearer his bowels,
And his nose were a pecker instead.'
1941

There was a young pair from Uganda
Who were having a f*** on a veranda.
The drip from their f***s
Fed forty-two ducks,
Three geese, and a f***ing big gander.
1942

There was a young man from Oswego
Who fell in love with a Dago.
He dreamt that his Venus
Was jerking his penis,
And woke up all covered with sago.
1946

There once was a baker of Nottingham
Who in making éclairs would put snot in 'em.
When he ran out of snot,
He would, like as not,
Take his pecker and jack off a shot in 'em.
1941

In the city of York there's a lass
Who will hitch up her dress when you pass.
If you toss her two bits
She will strip to the tits,
And let you explore her bare ass.
1945

There was an old spinster named Campbell
Got tangled one day in a bramble.
She cried, 'Ouch, how it sticks!
But so many sharp pricks
Are not met every day on a ramble.'

There once was a husky young Viking
Whose sexual prowess was striking.
Every time he got hot
He would scour the twat
Of some girl that might be to his liking.
1947

Two pretty young twins named Mahoney
Once tickled a horse's baloney.
With a spurt and a splash
They fell with a crash,
And no one knew which had the Toni.
1952

A Bavarian dame named Brunhilda
Went to bed with a jerry-built builder.
The end of his john
Was so badly put on
That it snapped in her bladder and killed her.
1941

There once was a priest of Gibraltar
Who wrote dirty jokes in his psalter.
An inhibited nun
Who had read every one
Made a vow to be laid on his altar.
1938

There once was a man from Nantucket
Whose dick was so long he could suck it.
He said, 'Though quite crass,'
As he lubed up his ass,
'I found a nice place I can tuck it.'

There was a young lady named Nance
Whose lover had St Vitus Dance.
When she dove for his prick,
He wriggled so quick,
She bit a piece out of his pants.
1941

There was a young lady named Nance
Who had ants in the seat of her pants.
When they bit her on bottom
She yelled, 'Jesus God rot 'em!
I can't do the St Vitus dance.'
1942

There was a young lady named Nance
Who learned about f***ing in France,
And when you'd insert it
She'd squeeze till she hurt it,
And shove it right back in your pants.
1951

A homely old spinster of France,
Who all the men looked at askance,
Threw her skirt overhead
And then jumped into bed,
Saying, 'Now I've at least half a chance.'
1941

A mystical painter named Foxx
Once picked up a girl on the docks.
He made an elliptic
Mysterious triptych,
And painted it right on her box.
1941

The Marquesa de Excusador
Used to pee on the drawing-room floor,
For the can was too cold
And when one grows old
To be much alone is a bore.
1942

There was a young girl from St Cyr
Whose reflex reactions were queer.
Her escort said, 'Mabel,
Get up off the table;
The money's to pay for the beer.'
1949

Said a meaty young woman of Croft,
Amusing herself in the loft,
'A salami or wurst
Is what I should choose first –
With bologna you know you've been boffed.'
1941

There was a young girl, very sweet,
Who thought sailors' meat quite a treat.
When she sat on their lap
She unbuttoned their flap.
And always had plenty to eat.
1944

There was a young fellow named Hyde
Who took a girl out for a ride.
He mucked up her f***-hole
And f***ed up her muck-hole,
And charged her two dollars beside.
1941

A frugal young fellow named Wise
Gets the most from the dead whores he buys.
After sporting a while
As a gay necrophile,
For dessert he has maggot surprise.
1941

There was a young couple named Kelly
Who had to live belly to belly,
Because once, in their haste,
They used library paste
Instead of petroleum jelly.
1938

There was a young fellow named Bouch
Who inveigled a girl to a couch.
He said, 'Pretty young miss,
I will take you, I wiss,
Horizontally, vertically, crouch.'
1945

There was a young girl of Cohoes
Who jerked herself off with her nose.
She said, 'Yes, I done it,
But just for the fun it
Afforded the folk of Cohoes.'

There was an old man from Pinole
Who always got in the wrong hole,
And when he withdrew,
All covered with goo,
His temper was out of control.
1942

There was a young fellow named Oakum
Whose brags about f***ing were hokum,
For he really preferred
To suck cocks and stir turd –
He was Queen of the Flits in Hoboken.
1941

There was a young girl from Sofire
Who succumbed to her lover's desire.
She said, 'It's a sin,
But now that it's in,
Could you shove it a few inches higher?'
1945

Beneath a tree one rainy day,
A lover and his swooning lady lay.
He was in her to the hilt,
And though she was nearly kilt,
She loved it, and kept hollering, 'Hooray!'
1941

A young man of Llanfairpwllgwyngyll
While bent over plucking a dingle
Had the whole Eisteddfod
Taking turns at his pod
While they sang some impossible jingle.
1952

Prince Absalom lay with his sister
And bundled and nibbled and kissed her,
But the kid was so tight,
And it was deep night,
Though he shot at the target, he missed her.
1942

There was a young girl named Regina
Who called in a water-diviner,
To play a slick trick
With his prick as a stick,
To help her locate her vagina.
1944

There once was an artist named Thayer
Who was really a cubist for fair.
He looked all his life
To find him a wife
Possessed of a c*** that was square.
1952

There was an old person of Gosham
Who took out his ballocks to wash 'em.
His wife said, 'Now, Jack,
If you don't put them back,
I'll step on your scrotum and squash 'em.'
1938

There was a young girl named Venus
Who had never encountered a penis.
When Van Stone threw his in
It went up to her chin,
But the bore, not the stroke, was the meanest.
1945

There was a young man from Split
Who was thrilled with the thought of shit.
He was simply elated,
Till he grew constipated,
But that took all the pleasure from it.
1943

There was a young lady of Ghat
Who never could sit but she shat.
Oh, the seat of her drawers
Was a chamber of horrors,
And they felt even fouler than that!
1941

No one can tell about Myrtle
Whether she's sterile or fertile.
If anyone tries
To tickle her thighs
She closes them tight like a turtle.
1943

There was an old spinster named Gretel
Who wore underclothes made of metal.
When they said, 'Does it hurt?'
She said, 'It keeps dirt
From stamen and pistil and petal.'
1942

There was a young girl named McKnight
Who got drunk with her boyfriend one night.
She came to in bed
With a split maidenhead –
That's the last time she ever was tight.
1941

The Bishop of Ibu Plantation
Wrote a thesis on Transfiguration
For the Christian Review
(As good Bishops do)
Whilst practising miscegenation.
1944

There was a young girl from Seattle
Who got her kicks sucking off cattle,
'til a bull from the South
Popped a load in her mouth
That made both her ovaries rattle.

There once was a gay young Parisian
Who came to an awful decision:
For his sexual joys
He'd have women and boys,
And snakes too, and no supervision!
1941

There once was a horny old bitch
With a motorized self-f***er which
She would use with delight
All day long and all night,
Twenty bucks: Abercrombie & Fitch.
1941

There was a young fellow of Mayence
Who f***ed his own arse, in defiance
Not only of custom
And morals, dad-bust him,
But most of the known laws of science.
1949

The woman who lives on the moon
Is still cherishing the balloon
Of an earthling who'd come
And given her some,
But had dribbled away all too soon.
1942

There once was a man of Belfast
Whose balls out of iron were cast.
He'd managed somehow
To bugger a sow,
Thus you get pig iron, at last.
1947

A person of most any nation
If afflicted with bad constipation,
Can shove a cuirass
Up the crack of his ass,
But it isn't a pleasing sensation.
1941

There was an old priest of Penang,
Wound barbed wire round his whang.
When they asked, 'Why'd you do it?'
The priest said, 'Oh, screw it!
It's just for the young girls I bang.'
1941

There once was a chick less than meek,
Who wished above all to be chic.
She thought it much neater
(Not to mention discreeter)
To do it with a sheik with a 'Sheik.'
1942

There once was a fellow named Glantz
Who on entering a toilet in France,
Was in such a heat
To paper the seat,
He shit right into his pants.
1941

SEX AND THE BAWDY LIMERICK

The grand-niece of Madame DuBarry
Suspected her son was a fairy.
'It's peculiar,' said she,
'But he sits down to pee,
And stands when I bathe the canary.'
1944

There was a young lady named Hall
Who went to a birth-control ball.
She was loaded with pessaries
And other accessories,
But no one approached her at all.
1938

There was a young lady from Ongar,
Got shagged in the sea, by a conger;
Her girlfriend from Deal
Asked, 'How did it feel?'
She said, 'Nice – Like a bloke – only longer!'

To the shrine which was Pallas Athena's
Young Bito (who'd learned about penis)
Brought her needles and thread
And scissors and said,
'You can stick them – I'm changing to Venus!'
1942

A synod of Anglican friars
Were discussing their carnal desires.
Said the priest from Tulagi,
'The Marys are baggy,
But a coconut truly inspires.'
1944

There was a young girl named O'Malley
Who wanted to dance in the ballet.
She got roars of applause
When she kicked off her drawers,
But her hair and her bush didn't tally.
1941

There was a young lady of Alnwicke
Whom a stranger threw into a panic.
For he frigged her and f***ed her,
And buggered and sucked her,
With a glee hardly short of satanic.
1941

There was a young girl whose divinity
Preserved her in perfect virginity,
'Til a candle, her nemesis,
Caused parthenogenesis –
Now she thinks herself one of the Trinity.
1943

A chap down in Oklahoma
Had a cock that could sing La Paloma,
But the sweetness of pitch
Couldn't put off the hitch
Of impotence, size and aroma.
1952

A pederast living in Arles
Used to bugger the bung of a barrel,
But was heard to lament,
'In the old days I went
Up the blue-blooded bum of an earl!'
1942

There was a pianist named Liszt
Who played with one hand while he pissed,
But as he grew older
His technique grew bolder,
And in concert jacked off with his fist.
1942

Some night when you're drunk on Dutch Bols
Try changing the usual roles.
The backward position
Is nice for coition
And it offers the choice of two holes.
1947

A young man from the banks of the Po
Found his cock had elongated so,
That when he'd pee
It was not he
But only his neighbours who'd know.
1944

There was a young genius in Texas
Who could flex his own solar plexus.
It made his ding bounce,
And he caught every ounce
Of his magical spraying of sexus.
1952

There was a young lady of Norway
Who hung by her heels in the doorway.
She said to her beau,
'Hey, look at me, Joe,
I think I've discovered one more way.'
1952

HOW THE LIMERICK BEGAN

At the best estimate, the limerick has been with us for about 180-plus years.

In this chapter are two sets of poems, '16 Stories of Women' and '15 Stories of Men', which appeared in London in 1820 and are among the first pieces that could be described as limericks.

This chapter also features the work of Edward Lear, who turned the limerick into an art form, 25 years after the first limericks were written. He wrote more than 100 limericks, which were published in two books in 1846 and 1855, although he preferred to call them 'Nonsense'. Each one came with one of his own masterful illustrations, and they proved immediately popular and enduring.

This chapter also contains contributions by Lewis Carroll, the writer of *Alice's Adventures In Wonderland*, Robert Louis Stevenson, who wrote adventure stories, and humorist Gellett Burgess.

1820s LIMERICKS

Edward Lear turned the limerick into an art form, with the publication of his first book, *A Book of Nonsense*, in 1846. But the style of telling a story through the limerick was already developing prior to Lear's writing.

Here are two groups of stories that were published in books in London in the 1820s. The first is '16 Stories of Women', the author of which is unknown, and the second is '15 Stories of Men', the author believed to be Richard Sharpe, a grocer from Bishopsgate.

16 Stories of Women

There was an Old Woman named Towl
Who went out to Sea with her Owl,
But the Owl was Sea-sick
And scream'd for Physic;
Which sadly annoy'd Mistress Towl.

There was an Old Woman at Gloster,
Whose parrot two guineas it cost her;
But his tongue never ceasing,
Was vastly displeasing
To that talkative Woman of Gloster.

There was an old woman of Ealing,
She jump'd till her head touch'd the ceiling;
When 2 1 6 4
Was announc'd at her door,
As a prize to th' Old Woman of Ealing.

There was an Old Woman of Norwich,
Who liv'd on nothing but porridge,
Parading the town,
She turned cloak into gown,
That thrifty Old Woman of Norwich.

There was an Old Woman of Harrow,
Who visited in a Wheel barrow,
And her servant before,
Knock'd loud at each door;
To announce the Old Woman of Harrow.

There was an Old Woman of Croydon,
To look young she affected the Hoyden,
And would jump and would skip,
Till she put out her hip;
Alas poor Old Woman of Croydon.

There was an Old woman of Gosport,
And she was one of the cross sort,
While she dress'd for the ball,
Her wig was too small;
Which enrag'd this Old Lady of Gosport.

There was an Old Woman of Leith,
Who had a sad pain in her Teeth,
But the Blacksmith uncouth,
Scar'd the pain from her tooth;
Which rejoic'd the Old Woman of Leith.

There came an Old Woman from France,
Who taught grown up Children to dance,
But they were so stiff,
She sent them home in a miff,
This sprightly Old Woman from France.

There was an Old Woman of Surrey,
Who was morn noon and night, in a hurry,
Call'd her husband a Fool,
Drove her children to school;
The worrying Old Woman of Surrey.

There dwelt an Old Woman Exeter,
When visitors came it sore vexed her,
So for fear they should eat,
She lock'd up all the meat;
This stingy Old Woman of Exeter.

There was an Old woman of Bath,
And she was as thin as a Lath,
She was brown as a berry,
With a Nose like a Cherry;
This skinny Old Woman of Bath.

There was an Old Woman in Spain,
To be civil went much 'gainst the grain,
Yet she danc'd a fandango,
With General Fernando;
This whimsical Woman of Spain.

There was an Old Woman of Leeds,
Who spent all her life in Good Deeds,
She work'd for the poor,
Till her fingers were sore,
This pious Old Woman of Leeds.

There was an Old Woman of Devon,
Who rose every morning at seven,
For her house to provide,
And to warm her inside;
This provident Woman of Devon.

There liv'd an Old Woman at Lynn,
Whose Nose very near touch'd her chin,
You may easy suppose,
She had plenty of Beaux;
This charming Old Woman of Lynn.

15 Stories of Men

As a little fat man of Bombay
Was smoking one very hot day,
A bird called a Snipe,
Flew away with his pipe,
Which vex'd the fat man of Bombay.

A merry old man of Oporto,
Had long had the gout in his fore toe;
And oft when he spoke
To relate a good joke,
A terrible twinge cut it short O!

Said a very proud Farmer at Rye-gate,
When the Squire rode up to his high gate,
With your horse and your hound,
You had better go round,
For, I say, you shan't jump over my gate.

There was a rich Squire of Southwark,
From morning to night did his mouth work,
So much and so fast,
That he greatly surpass'd,
Westminster, London and Southwark.

There was an old captain of Dover,
Whom all the physicians gave over;
At the sound of the drum
And 'The enemy's come'
Up jump'd the bold captain of Dover.

A butcher there was at Athlone,
Whom a beggar once ask'd for a bone;
But he drove him away
With a blow of his tray –
O! his heart was as hard as a stone.

There was a young man at St. Kitts,
Who was very much troubled with fits;
An eclipse of the moon
Threw him into a swoon;
Alas! poor young man of St. Kitts.

A Tailor who sailed from Quebec,
In a storm ventur'd once upon deck,
But the waves of the sea,
Were as strong as could be,
And he tumbled in up to his neck.

There was an Old Miser at Reading,
Had a house, with a yard with a shed in,
'Twas meant for a cow,
But so small that I vow,
The poor creature could scarce get its head in.

There was an old soldier of Bicester,
Was walking one day with his sister,
A bull, with one poke,
Toss'd her into an oak,
Before the old gentleman miss'd her.

There was a sick man of Tobago,
Liv'd long on rice-gruel and sago;
But at last to his bliss,
The physician said this –
'To a roast leg of mutton you may go.'

An old gentleman living at Harwich,
At ninety was thinking of marriage,
In came his grandson,
Who was just twenty-one,
And went off with the bride in his carriage.

There was a poor man of Jamaica,
He open'd a shop as a baker;
The nice biscuits he made
Procured him much trade,
With the little black boys of Jamaica.

A lively old man at Madeira,
Thought that wine of the heart was a cheerer,
He often would say,
'Put the bottle this way –
Absent friends! – and I wish they were nearer.'

There was an old merchant at Malta,
Very cross but too stubborn to alter,
He flew in a rage
With poor Dr Sage,
Who attended sick people at Malta.

EDWARD LEAR

The Man who Made the Limerick

Edward Lear, the man who popularised the limerick, was a remarkable character right from the start. Born in London in 1812, he was the 20th child of a stockbroker! However, his father fell on hard times and Edward was brought up by his sister Ann. He suffered from epilepsy and depression, yet he was an artist and painter of such skill that he collaborated on books with John Gould, the famous expert on birds.

A much travelled man, Lear turned to writing and his sense of humour emerged in his collection of self-penned limericks, *A Book of Nonsense*, published in 1846, under the pseudonym, Derry Down Derry.

He would never claim to be the inventor of the limerick. And as some 1820s limericks printed elsewhere in this book reveal, the style of writing was already gaining popularity. But Lear developed it into something special, aided by his clever drawings that supported each story.

His second volume appeared in 1855, and even more limericks were published. In this chapter are the complete works from the first two books, plus some others.

The notable difference to the limerick is that Lear's style saw the fifth line usually being merely a repeat or a slight variation of the first line – invariably, the final word in the first and fifth lines was the same. These days, of course, the fifth line has become the real punch line, with a new rhyming word providing the 'twist', a concept that began to develop a few years after Lear set the benchmark.

Lear wrote other books of 'Nonsense', songs, lyrics and pictures, among more serious works on travel and illustrating zoology books. He died in Italy in 1888.

Here are Lear's original 'Nonsense' poems:

There was an Old Man with a beard,
Who said, 'It is just as I feared!
Two Owls and a Hen,
Four Larks and a Wren,
Have all built their nests in my beard!'

There was a Young Lady of Ryde,
Whose shoe-strings were seldom untied.
She purchased some clogs,
And some small spotted dogs,
And frequently walked about Ryde.

There was an Old Man with a nose,
Who said, 'If you choose to suppose,
That my nose is too long,
You are certainly wrong!'
That remarkable Man with a nose.

There was an Old Man on a hill,
Who seldom, if ever, stood still;
He ran up and down,
In his Grandmother's gown,
Which adorned that Old Man on a hill.

There was a Young Lady whose bonnet,
Came untied when the birds sate upon it;
But she said: 'I don't care!
All the birds in the air
Are welcome to sit on my bonnet!'

There was a Young Person of Smyrna,
Whose Grandmother threatened to burn her;
But she seized on the cat,
And said, 'Granny, burn that!
You incongruous Old Woman of Smyrna!'

There was an Old Person of Chili,
Whose conduct was painful and silly,
He sate on the stairs,
Eating apples and pears,
That imprudent Old Person of Chili.

There was an Old Man with a gong,
Who bumped at it all day long;
But they called out, 'O law!
You're a horrid old bore!'
So they smashed that Old Man with a gong.

There was an Old Lady of Chertsey,
Who made a remarkable curtsey;
She twirled round and round,
Till she sunk underground,
Which distressed all the people of Chertsey.

There was an Old Man in a tree,
Who was horribly bored by a Bee;
When they said, 'Does it buzz?'
He replied, 'Yes, it does!
It's a regular brute of a Bee!'

There was an Old Man with a flute,
A sarpint ran into his boot;
But he played day and night,
Till the sarpint took flight,
And avoided that man with a flute.

There was a Young Lady whose chin,
Resembled the point of a pin;
So she had it made sharp,
And purchased a harp,
And played several tunes with her chin.

There was an Old Man of Kilkenny,
Who never had more than a penny;
He spent all that money,
In onions and honey,
That wayward Old Man of Kilkenny.

There was an Old Person of Ischia,
Whose conduct grew friskier and friskier;
He dance hornpipes and jigs,
And ate thousands of figs,
That lively Old Person of Ischia.

There was an Old Man in a boat,
Who said, 'I'm afloat, I'm afloat!'
When they said, 'No! you ain't!'
He was ready to faint,
That unhappy Old Man in a boat.

There was a Young Lady of Portugal,
Whose ideas were excessively nautical:
She climbed up a tree,
To examine the sea,
But declared she would never leave Portugal.

There was an Old Man of Moldavia,
Who had the most curious behaviour;
For while he was able,
He slept on a table.
That funny Old Man of Moldavia.

There was an Old Man of Madras,
Who rode on a cream-coloured ass;
But the length of its ears,
So promoted his fears,
That it killed that Old Man of Madras.

There was an Old Person of Leeds,
Whose head was infested with beads;
She sat on a stool,
And ate gooseberry fool,
Which agreed with that person of Leeds.

There was an Old Man of Peru,
Who never knew what he should do;
So he tore off his hair,
And behaved like a bear,
That intrinsic Old Man of Peru.

There was an Old Person of Hurst,
Who drank when he was not athirst;
When they said, 'You'll grow fatter,'
He answered, 'What matter?'
That globular Person of Hurst.

There was a Young Person of Crete,
Whose toilette was far from complete;
She dressed in a sack,
Spickle-speckled with black,
That ombliferous person of Crete.

There was on Old Man of the Isles,
Whose face was pervaded with smiles;
He sung high dum diddle,
And played on the fiddle,
That amiable Man of the Isles.

There was an Old Person of Buda,
Whose conduct grew ruder and ruder;
Till at last, with a hammer,
They silenced his clamour,
By smashing that Person of Buda.

There was an Old Man of Columbia,
Who was thirsty, and called out for some beer;
But they brought it quite hot,
In a small copper pot,
Which disgusted that man of Columbia.

There was a Young Lady of Dorking,
Who bought a large bonnet for walking;
But its colour and size,
So bedazzled her eyes,
That she very soon went back to Dorking.

There was an Old Man who supposed,
That the street door was partially closed;
But some very large rats,
Ate his coats and his hats,
While that futile old gentleman dozed.

There was an Old Man of the West,
Who wore a pale plum-coloured vest;
When they said, 'Does it fit?'
He replied, 'Not a bit!'
That uneasy Old Man of the West.

There was an Old Man of the Wrekin
Whose shoes made a horrible creaking
But they said, 'Tell us whether,
Your shoes are of leather,
Or of what, you Old Man of the Wrekin?'

There was a Young Lady whose eyes,
Were unique as to colour and size;
When she opened them wide,
People all turned aside,
And started away in surprise.

There was a Young Lady of Norway,
Who casually sat on a doorway;
When the door squeezed her flat,
She exclaimed, 'What of that?'
This courageous Young Lady of Norway.

There was an Old Man of Vienna,
Who lived upon Tincture of Senna;
When that did not agree,
He took Camomile Tea,
That nasty Old Man of Vienna.

There was an Old Person whose habits,
Induced him to feed upon rabbits;
When he'd eaten eighteen,
He turned perfectly green,
Upon which he relinquished those habits.

There was an Old Person of Dover,
Who rushed through a field of blue Clover;
But some very large bees,
Stung his nose and his knees,
So he very soon went back to Dover.

There was an Old Man of Marseilles,
Whose daughters wore bottle-green veils;
They caught several Fish,
Which they put in a dish,
And sent to their Pa' at Marseilles.

There was an Old Person of Cadiz,
Who was always polite to all ladies;
But in handing his daughter,
He fell into the water,
Which drowned that Old Person of Cadiz.

There was an Old Person of Basing,
Whose presence of mind was amazing;
He purchased a steed,
Which he rode at full speed,
And escaped from the people of Basing.

There was an Old Man of Quebec,
A beetle ran over his neck;
But he cried, 'With a needle,
I'll slay you, O beadle!'
That angry Old Man of Quebec.

There was an Old Person of Philæ,
Whose conduct was scroobious and wily;
He rushed up a Palm,
When the weather was calm,
And observed all the ruins of Philæ.

The was a Young Lady of Bute,
Who played on a silver-gilt flute;
She played several jigs,
To her uncle's white pigs,
That amusing Young Lady of Bute.

There was a Young Lady whose nose,
Was so long that it reached to her toes;
So she hired an Old Lady,
Whose conduct was steady,
To carry that wonderful nose.

There was a Young Lady of Turkey,
Who wept when the weather was murky;
When the day turned out fine,
She ceased to repine,
That capricious Young Lady of Turkey.

There was an Old Man of Apulia,
Whose conduct was very peculiar
He fed twenty sons,
Upon nothing but buns,
That whimsical Man of Apulia.

There was an Old Man with a poker,
Who painted his face with red ochre
When they said, 'You're a Guy!'
He made no reply,
But knocked them all down with his poker.

There was an Old Person of Prague,
Who was suddenly seized with the Plague;
But they gave him some butter,
Which caused him to mutter,
And cured that Old Person of Prague.

There was an Old Man of the North,
Who fell into a basin of broth;
But a laudable cook,
Fished him out with a hook,
Which saved that Old Man of the North.

There was a Young Lady of Poole,
Whose soup was excessively cool;
So she put it to boil
By the aid of some oil,
That ingenious Young Lady of Poole.

There was an Old Person of Mold,
Who shrank from sensations of cold,
So he purchased some muffs,
Some furs and some fluffs,
And wrapped himself from the cold.

There was an Old Man of Nepaul,
From his horse had a terrible fall;
But, though split quite in two,
By some very strong glue,
They mended that Man of Nepaul.

There was an Old Man of th'Abruzzi,
So blind that he couldn't his foot see;
When they said, 'That's your toe,'
He replied, 'Is it so?'
That doubtful Old Man of th'Abruzzi.

There was an Old Person of Rhodes,
Who strongly objected to toads;
He paid several cousins,
To catch them by the dozens,
That futile Old Person of Rhodes.

There was an Old Man of Peru,
Who watched his wife making a stew;
But once by mistake,
In a stove she did bake,
That unfortunate Man of Peru.

There was an Old Man of Melrose,
Who walked on the tips of his toes;
But they said, 'It ain't pleasant,
To see you at present,
You stupid Old Man of Melrose.'

There was a Young Lady of Lucca,
Whose lovers completely forsook her;
She ran up a tree,
And said, 'Fiddle-de-dee!'
Which embarrassed the people of Lucca.

There was an Old Man of Bohemia,
Whose daughter was christened Euphemia,
Till one day, to his grief,
She married a thief,
Which grieved that Old Man of Bohemia.

There was an Old Man of Vesuvius,
Who studied the works of Vitruvius;
When the flames burnt his book,
To drinking he took,
That morbid Old Man of Vesuvius.

There was an Old Man of Cape Horn,
Who wished he had never been born;
So he sat on a chair,
Till he died of despair,
That dolorous Man of Cape Horn.

There was an Old Lady whose folly,
Induced her to sit on a holly;
Whereon by a thorn,
Her dress being torn,
She quickly became melancholy.

There was an Old Man of Corfu,
Who never knew what he should do;
So he rushed up and down,
Till the sun made him brown,
That bewildered Old Man of Corfu.

There was an Old Man of the South,
Who had an immoderate mouth;
But in swallowing a dish,
That was quite full of fish,
He was choked, that Old Man of the South.

There was an Old Man of the Nile,
Who sharpened his nails with a file,
Till he cut out his thumbs,
And said calmly, 'This comes
Of sharpening one's nails with a file!'

There was an Old Person of Rheims,
Who was troubled with horrible dreams;
So, to keep him awake
They fed him on cake,
Which amused that Old Person of Rheims.

There was an Old Person of Cromer,
Who stood on one leg to read Homer;
When he found he grew stiff,
He jumped over the cliff,
Which concluded that Person of Cromer.

There was an old person of Troy,
Whose drink was warm brandy and soy,
Which he took with a spoon,
By the light of the moon,
In sight of the city of Troy.

There was an Old Man of the Dee,
Who was sadly annoyed by a flea;
When he said, 'I will scratch it,'
They gave him a hatchet,
Which grieved that Old Man of the Dee.

There was an Old Man of Dundee,
Who frequented the top of a tree;
When disturbed by the crows,
He abruptly arose,
And exclaimed, 'I'll return to Dundee.'

There was an Old Person of Tring,
Who embellished his nose with a ring;
He gazed at the moon
Every evening in June,
That ecstatic Old Person in Tring.

There was an Old Man on some rocks,
Who shut his wife up in a box;
When she said, 'Let me out!'
He exclaimed, 'Without doubt,
You will pass all your life in that box.'

There was an Old Man of Coblenz,
The length of whose legs was immense;
He went with one prance
From Turkey to France,
That surprising Old Man of Coblenz.

There was an Old Man of Calcutta,
Who perpetually ate bread and butter,
Till a great bit of muffin,
On which he was stuffing,
Choked that horrid Old Man of Calcutta.

There was an Old Man in a pew,
Whose waistcoat was spotted with blue;
But he tore it in pieces
To give to his nieces,
That cheerful Old Man in a pew.

There was an Old Man who said, 'How
Shall I flee from that horrible cow?
I will sit on this stile,
And continue to smile,
Which may soften the heart of that cow.'

There was a Young Lady of Hull,
Who was chased by a virulent bull;
But she seized on a spade,
And called out, 'Who's afraid?'
Which distracted that virulent bull.

There was an Old Man of Whitehaven,
Who danced a quadrille with a raven;
But they said, 'It's absurd
To encourage this bird!'
So they smashed that Old Man of Whitehaven.

There was an Old Man of Leghorn,
The smallest that ever was born;
But quickly snapped up he
Was once by a puppy,
Who devoured that Old Man of Leghorn.

There was an Old Man of the Hague,
Whose ideas were excessively vague;
He built a balloon
To examine the moon,
That deluded Old Man of the Hague.

There was an Old Man of Jamaica,
Who suddenly married a Quaker;
But she cried out, 'Alack!
I have married a black!'
Which distressed that Old Man of Jamaica.

There was an Old Person of Dutton,
Whose head was as small as a button,
So, to make it look big,
He purchased a wig,
And rapidly rushed about Dutton.

There was a Young Lady of Tyre,
Who swept the loud chords of a lyre;
At the sound of each sweep
She enraptured the deep,
And enchanted the city of Tyre.

There was an Old Man who said, 'Hush!
I perceive a young bird in this bush!'
When they said, 'Is it small?'
He replied, 'Not at all!
It is four times as big as the bush!'

There was an Old Man of the East,
Who gave all his children a feast;
But they all ate so much
And their conduct was such
That it killed that Old Man of the East.

There was an Old Man of Kamschatka,
Who possessed a remarkable fat cur;
His gait and his waddle
Were held as a model
To all the fat dogs in Kamschatka.

There was an Old Man of the coast,
Who placidly sat on a post;
But when it was cold
He relinquished his hold
And called for some hot buttered toast.

There was an Old Person of Bangor,
Whose face was distorted with anger!
He tore off his boots,
And subsisted on roots,
That irascible Person of Bangor.

There was an Old Man with a beard,
Who sat on a horse when he reared;
But they said, 'Never mind!
You will fall off behind,
You propitious Old Man with a beard!'

There was an Old Man of the West,
Who never could get any rest;
So they set him to spin
On his nose and chin,
Which cured that Old Man of the West.

There was an Old Person of Anerley,
Whose conduct was strange and unmannerly;
He rushed down the Strand
With a pig in each hand,
But returned in the evening to Anerley.

There was a Young Lady of Troy,
Whom several large flies did annoy;
Some she killed with a thump,
Some she drowned at the pump,
And some she took with her to Troy.

There was an Old Person of Berlin,
Whose form was uncommonly thin;
Till he once, by mistake,
Was mixed up in a cake,
So they baked that Old Man of Berlin.

There was an Old Person of Spain,
Who hated all trouble and pain;
So he sat on a chair,
With his feet in the air,
That umbrageous Old Person of Spain.

There was a Young Lady of Russia,
Who screamed so that no one could hush her;
Her screams were extreme, –
No one heard such a scream
As was screamed by that Lady from Russia.

There was an Old Man who said, 'Well!
Will nobody answer this bell?
I have pulled day and night,
Till my hair has grown white,
But nobody answers this bell!'

There was a Young Lady of Wales,
Who caught a large fish without scales;
When she lifted her hook
She exclaimed, 'Only look!'
That ecstatic Young Lady of Wales.

There was an Old Person of Cheadle,
Who was put in the stocks by the beadle
For stealing some pigs,
Some coats, and some wigs,
That horrible person of Cheadle.

There was a Young Lady of Welling,
Whose praise all the world was a-telling;
She played on a harp,
And caught several carp,
That accomplished Young Lady of Welling.

There was an Old Person of Tartary,
Who divided his jugular artery;
But he screeched to his wife,
And she said, 'Oh, my life!
Your death will be felt by all Tartary!'

There was an Old Person of Chester,
Whom several small children did pester;
They threw some large stones,
Which broke most of his bones,
And displeased that Old Person of Chester.

There was an Old Man with a owl,
Who continued to bother and howl;
He sat on a rail
And imbibed bitter ale,
Which refreshed that Old Man and his owl.

There was an Old Person from Gretna,
Who rushed down the crater of Etna;
When they said, 'Is it hot?'
He replied, 'No, it's not!'
That mendacious Old Person of Gretna.

There was a Young Lady of Sweden,
Who went by the slow rain to Weedon;
When they cried, 'Weedon Station!'
She made no observation
But thought she should go back to Sweden.

There was a Young Girl of Majorca,
Whose aunt was a very fast walker;
She walked seventy miles,
And leaped fifteen stiles,
Which astonished that Girl of Majorca.

There was an Old Man of the Cape,
Who possessed a large Barbary ape,
Till the ape one dark night
Set the house all alight,
Which burned that Old Man of the Cape.

There was an Old Lady of Prague,
Whose language was horribly vague;
When they said, 'Are these caps?'
She answered, 'Perhaps!'
That oracular Lady of Prague.

There was an Old Person of Sparta,
Who had twenty-one sons and one 'darter';
He fed them on snails,
And weighed them in scales,
That wonderful Person of Sparta.

There was an Old Man at a casement,
Who held up his hands in amazement;
When they said, 'Sir, you'll fall!'
He replied, 'Not at all!'
That incipient Old Man at a casement.

There was an Old Person of Burton,
Whose answers were rather uncertain;
When they said, 'How d'ye do?'
He replied, 'Who are you?'
That distressing Old Person of Burton.

There was an Old Person of Ems,
Who casually fell in the Thames;
And when he was found
They said he was drowned,
That unlucky Old Person of Ems.

There was an Old Person of Ewell,
Who chiefly subsisted on gruel;
But to make it more nice
He inserted some mice,
Which refreshed that Old Person of Ewell.

There was a Young Lady of Parma,
Whose conduct grew calmer and calmer;
When they said, 'Are you dumb?'
She merely said, 'Hum!'
That provoking Young Lady of Parma.

There was an Old Man of Aôsta,
Who possessed a large cow, but he lost her;
But they said, 'Don't you see
She has rushed up a tree?
You invidious Old Man of Aôsta!'

There was an Old Man, on whose nose,
Most birds of the air could repose;
But they all flew away
At the closing of day,
Which relieved that Old Man and his nose.

There was a Young Lady of Clare,
Who was sadly pursued by a bear;
When she found she was tired,
She abruptly expired,
That unfortunate Lady of Clare.

There was an Old Man of Kildare,
Who climbed into a very old chair;
When he said, – 'Here I stays,
Till the end of my days,'
That immovable Man of Kildare.

There was an Old Man of New York,
Who murdered himself with a fork;
But nobody cried,
Though he very soon died,
For that silly Old Man of New York.

There was an Old Sailor of Compton,
Whose vessel a rock it once bump'd on;
The shock was so great,
That it damaged the pate,
Of that singular Sailor of Compton.

There was a young lady of Greenwich
Whose garments were bordered with spinach
But a large spotty calf
Bit her shawl quite in half
Which alarmed that young lady of Greenwich.

There was a young lady in blue,
Who said, 'Is it you? Is it You?'
When they said, 'Yes, it is,'
She replied only 'Whizz!'
That ungracious lady in blue.

There was an old man, who when little
Fell casually into a kettle;
But, growing too stout
He could never get out,
So he passed all his life in that kettle.

There was an old person of Anerly,
Who conduct was strange and unmannerly;
He rushed down the strand
With a pig in each hand,
But returned in the evening to Anerly.

There was an old person of Ware
Who rode on the back of a bear;
When they said, 'Does it trot?'
He said: 'Certainly not,
It's a Moppsikon Floppsikon bear.'

There was an old person of Wick,
Who said, 'Tick-a-Tick, Tick-a-Tick,
Chickabee, Chickabaw,'
And he said nothing more,
This laconic old person of Wick.

There was an old person of Woking,
Whose mind was perverse and provoking;
He sat on a rail,
With his head in a pail,
That illusive old person of Woking.

There was an old man of Thermopylae,
Who never did anything properly;
But they said: 'If you choose
To boil eggs in your shoes,
You cannot remain in Thermopylae.'

Famous Writers

And their Contribution to the Limerick and its Variations

Edward Lear's popularisation of the limerick ultimately lead to writers usually known for their expertise in novels, children's books and music to try their hand at writing limericks also.

Such writers include Lewis Carroll, the author of *Alice's Adventures In Wonderland*, Robert Louis Stevenson, who wrote of life on the bounding main, and humorist Gellett Burgess.

Here are some samples of their work:

Lewis Carroll

Carroll was born Charles Lutwidge Dodgson on 27 January 1832 at Daresbury in Cheshire, England. He would have been in his early teens when Edward Lear's limericks were published.

Carroll wrote this limerick (and for those that don't know, a 'hod' is a bricklayer's portable device for carrying the essentials):

There was a young man of Oporta,
Who daily got shorter and shorter.
The reason he said
Was the hod on his head
Which was filled with the heaviest mortar.

Oliver Wendell Holmes

Holmes was a respected author who loved the incisiveness of the pun.

Among his writings:

The Reverend Henry Ward Beecher
Called a hen a most elegant creature.
The hen, pleased with that,
Laid an egg in his hat –
And thus did the hen reward Beecher.

Robert Louis Stevenson

Stevenson was born in Scotland in 1850. A writer of rollicking adventure yarns, particularly about pirates on the bounding main, he applied a geographical edge to his limericks:

There was an old man of the Cape
Who made himself garments of crepe.
When asked, 'Do they tear?'
He replied, 'Here and there;
But they're perfectly splendid for shape.'

When I was down beside the sea
A wooden spade they gave to me
To dig the sandy shore.
My holes were empty like a cup.
In every hole the sea came up,
Till it could come no more.

Rudyard Kipling
Kipling was better known for his serious poems and books, for example 'Kim', but his humour shows through in this limerick:

There once was a boy in Quebec,
Who was buried in snow to his neck.
When asked, 'Are you frizz?'
He replied, 'Yes, I is.
But we don't call this cold in Quebec.'

Gelett Burgess
Frank Gelett Burgess, born in 1866, was an American author and illustrator of popular humorous books.

One of his verses – not in the traditional five-line limerick style – was about the famous purple cow:

I never saw a purple cow
I never hope to see one
But I can tell you, anyhow,
I'd rather see than be one.

It became so popular, he even did a follow-up:

Ah yes! I wrote the 'Purple Cow'
I'm sorry, now, I wrote it!
But I can tell you, anyhow,
I'll kill you if you quote it!

He used this four-line style to effect in these two limericks:

The roof it has a lazy time
A-lying in the sun;
The walls, they have to hold him up;
They do not have much fun!

My feet they haul me round the house,
They hoist me up the stairs;
I only have to steer them, and
They ride me Everywheres!

Burgess also wrote some classic five-line limericks:

I wish that my room had a floor
I don't care so much for a door
But this walking around
Without touching the ground
Is getting to be quite a bore.

I'd rather have fingers than toes
I'd rather have ears than a nose
And as for my hair
I'm glad it's still there.
I'll be awfully sad when it goes.

But Burgess' best known limericks appeared in his series of books about bad-mannered children, called *Goops*, including *Goops And How to Be Them*, published in 1900. These were in limerick style, although not set out in the traditional five lines.

His most famous piece was 'An Alphabet of Famous Goops'. This is exactly how it was written by Burgess, capitals and all:

ABEDNEGO was Meek and Mild; he Softly Spoke, he
    Sweetly Smiled.
He never Called his Playmates Names, and he was Good in
    Running Games;
But he was Often in Disgrace because he had a Dirty Face!

BOHUNKUS would Take Off his Hat, and Bow and Smile,
    and Things like That.
His Face and Hair were Always Neat, and when he Played
    he did not Cheat;
But Oh! what Awful Words he Said, when it was Time to Go
    to Bed!

The Gentle CEPHAS tried his Best to Please his Friends
    with Merry Jest;
He tried to Help Them, when he Could, for CEPHAS, he was
    Very Good;
And Yet – They Say he Used to Cry, and Once or Twice he
    Told a Lie!

DANIEL and DAGO were a Pair who Acted Kindly
    Everywhere;
They studied Hard, as Good as Gold, they Always did as
    They were Told;
They Never Put on Silly Airs, but They Took Things that
    were Not Theirs.

EZEKIEL, so his Parents said, just Simply Loved to Go to Bed;
He was as Quiet as could Be whenever there were Folks to
  Tea;
And yet, he had a Little Way of Grumbling, when he should
  Obey.

When FESTUS was but Four Years Old his Parents Seldom
  had to Scold;
They never Called him 'FESTUS DON'T!' he Never Whined
  and said 'I Won't!'
Yet it was Sad to See him Dine. His Table Manners were Not
  Fine.

GAMALIEL took Peculiar Pride in Making Others Satisfied.
One Time I asked him for his Head. 'Why, Certainly!
  GAMALIEL Said.
He was Too Generous, in Fact. But Bravery he Wholly
  Lacked.

HAZAEL was (at Least he Said he Was) Exceedingly Well
  Bred;
Forbidden Sweets he would not Touch, though he might
  Want them very Much.
But Oh, Imagination Fails to quite Describe his Finger Nails!

How Interesting ISAAC Seemed! He never Fibbed, he
  Seldom Screamed;
His Company was Quite a Treat to all the Children on the
  Street;
But Nurse has Told me of his Wrath when he was Made to
  Take a Bath!

Oh, Think of JONAH when you're Bad; Think what a Happy
Way he had
Of Saying 'Thank You! – 'If you Please' – 'Excuse Me, Sir,' and
Words like These.
Still, he was Human, like Us All. His Muddy Footprints
Tracked the Hall.

Just fancy KADESH for a Name! Yet he was Clever All the
Same;
He knew Arithmetic, at Four, as Well as Boys of Nine or
More!
But I Prefer far Duller Boys, who do Not Make such Awful
Noise!

Oh, Laugh at LABAN, if you Will, but he was Brave when he
was Ill.
When he was Ill, he was so Brave he Swallowed All his
Mother Gave!
But Somehow, She could never Tell why he was Worse
when he was Well!

If MICAH's Mother Told him 'No' he Made but Little of his
Woe;
He Always Answered, 'Yes, I'll Try!' for MICAH Thought it
Wrong to Cry.
Yet he was Always Asking Questions and Making quite Ill-
timed Suggestions.

I Fancy NICODEMUS Knew as Much as I, or even You;
He was Too Careful, I am Sure, to Scratch or Soil the
  Furniture;
He never Squirmed, he never Squalled; he Never Came
  when he was Called!

Some think that OBADIAH'S Charm was that he Never
  Tried to Harm
Dumb Animals in any Way, though Some are Cruel when
  they Play.
But though he was so Sweet and Kind, his Mother found
  him Slow to Mind.

When PELEG had a Penny Earned, to Share it with his
  Friends he Yearned.
And if he Bought a Juicy Fig, his Sister's Half was Very Big!
Had he not Hated to Forgive, he would have been Too
  Good to Live!

When QUARTO'S brother QUARTO Hit, was QUARTO
  Angry? Not a Bit!
He Called the Blow a Little Joke, and so Affectionately
  Spoke,
That Everybody Loved the Lad. Yet Oh, What Selfish Ways
  he had!

Was REUBEN Happy? I should Say! He laughed and Sang
the Livelong Day.
He Made his Mother Smile with Joy to See her Sunny-
Tempered Boy.
However, she was Not so Gay when REUB Refused to Stop
his Play!

When SHADRACH Cared to be Polite, they Called him
Gentlemanly, Quite;
His Manners were Correct and Nice; he Never Asked for
Jelly Twice!
Still, when he Tried to Misbehave, O, how Much Trouble
SHADRACH Gave!

Don't Think that TIMOTHY was Ill because he Sometimes
Kept so Still.
He knew his Mother Did Not Care to Hear him Talking
Everywhere.
He did not Tease, he did Not Cry, but he was Always Asking
'WHY?'

URIAH Never Licked his Knife, nor Sucked his Fingers, in
his Life.
He Never Reached, to Help Himself, the Sugar Bowl upon
the Shelf.
He Never Popped his Cherry Pits; but he had Horrid Sulky
Fits!

To See young VIVIUS at his Work, you Knew he'd Never Try
to Shirk.
The Most Unpleasant Things he'd Do, if but his Mother
Asked him To.
But when young Vivius Grew Big, it Seems he was a Norful
Prig!

Why WABAN always Seemed so Sweet, was that he Kept so
Clean and Neat.
He never Smooched his Face with Coal, his Picture Books
were Fresh and Whole.
He washed His Hands Ten Times a Day; but, Oh, what
Horrid Words he'd Say!

What shall I say of XENOGOR, Save that he Always Shut the
Door!
He always Put his Toys Away when he had Finished with
his Play.
But here his List of Virtues Ends. A Tattle-Tale does not Make
Friends.

YERO was Noted for the Way with which he Helped his
Comrades Play;
He'd Lend his Cart, he'd Lend his Ball, his Marbles, and his
Tops and All!
And Yet (I Doubt if you' ll Believe), he Wiped his Nose upon
his Sleeve!

The Zealous ZIBEON was Such as Casual Callers Flatter
   Much.
His Maiden Aunts would Say, with Glee, 'How Good, how
   Pure, how Dear is He!'
And Yet, he Drove his Mother Crazy – he was so Slow, he
   was so Lazy!

Eugene Field

A skill of the accomplished limerick writer is to mix and
match the spelling of words with their phonetic pro-
nunciation. The 'Playing with Words' section in the Family
Limericks chapter has some excellent examples.

Eugene Field was one of the first to utilise the oppor-
tunities of this style, (please try to ignore the political
incorrectness):

Now, what in the world shall we dioux
With the bloody and murderous Sioux.
Who some time ago
Took an arrow and bow
And raised such a hellabelioux . . . ?

William Cosmo Monkhouse

Cosmo Monkhouse, a British poet, was a remarkable
character, who juggled a career in the civil service, in such
areas as trade, with his poetry. He came to the fore with
books including *A Dream of Idleness & Other Poems*.

He was also a prolific writer of limericks, many of which
have become classics through the ages, including this superb
piece:

There once was a lady of Niger,
Who smiled as she rode on a tiger.
They returned from the ride
With the lady inside –
And the smile on the face of the tiger.

Other gems from the pen of Monkhouse include:

A diner while dining at Crewe
Found a rather large mouse in his stew.
Said the waiter, 'Don't shout
And wave it about,
Or the rest will be wanting one too.'

There was a young lady named Laura,
Who went to the wilds of Angora,
She came back on a goat
With a beautiful coat,
And notes of the fauna and flora.

There once was a fellow from Clyde
Who once at a funeral was spied.
When asked who was dead
He smilingly said,
'I don't know, I just came for the ride.'

There once was an old monk of Basing,
Whose salads were something amazing;
But he told his confessor
That Nebuchadnezzar
Had given him hints upon grazing.

There was a composer named Liszt
Whose music no one could resistz.
When he swept the keyboard
Nobody could be bored
And now that he's gone he is miszd.

A glutton who came from the Rhine
When asked what hour he would dine,
Replied: 'At eleven,
At three, five, and seven,
And eight and a quarter past nine.'

There once was an old man of Lyme
Who married three wives at a time,
When asked, 'Why a third?'
He replied, 'One's absurd!
And bigamy, sir, is a crime.'

There was a young man from Laconia
Whose mother-in-law had pneumonia.
He hoped for the worst
And after March first
They buried her 'neath a begonia.

There was a young joker named Tarr
Who playfully pickled his ma.
When he finished his work
He remarked with a smirk,
'This will make quite a family jar.'

A reckless young man from Fort Blaney
Made love to a spinster named Janie.
When his friends said, 'Oh dear,
She's so old and so queer.'
He replied, 'But the day was so rainy.'

There was a young lady from Rye
With a shape like a capital I
When they said, 'It's too bad,'
She learned how to pad
Which shows you that figures can lie.

One of Monkhouse's gems was There Was an Old Man from
Nantucket:

There was an old man from Nantucket
Who kept all his cash in a bucket.
His daughter, named Nan,
Ran away with a man
And as for the bucket, Nantucket.

Many sequels that used the same or similar theme followed
the Nantucket limerick, such as:

He followed the pair to Pawtucket
The man and the girl with the bucket
And he said to the man
He was welcome to Nan
But as for the bucket, Pawtucket.

In fact, as seen in the Family Limericks chapter earlier in this book, the Nantucket idea became a challenge series between American newspapers.

Other Verse
Other verse of the same quirkiness, but not the same rhyme, includes:

I eat my peas with honey,
I've done it all my life:
It makes them taste quite funny,
But it keeps them on the knife.

As I was climbing up the stair
I met a man who wasn't there;
He wasn't there again to-day:
Oh, how I wish he'd go away!

Once there was an elephant,
Who tried to use the telephant –
No! No! I mean an elephone
Who tried to use the telephone –
(Dear me! I am not certain quite
That even now I've got it right.)

Howe'er it was, he got his trunk
Entangled in the telephunk;
The more he tried to get it free,
The louder buzzed the telephee –
(I fear I'd better drop the song
Of elephop and telephong!)

– Laura E. Richards (1850–1943)

'Twixt optimist and pessimist
The difference is droll
The optimist sees the doughnut
The pessimist sees the hole.
        – McLandburg Wilson, 1915

WS Gilbert

Gilbert was best known for writing the book and lyrics of the famous Gilbert & Sullivan light operas, collaborating with composer Sir Arthur Sullivan.

Gilbert's plays on words, and their ability to rhyme, still stand testament to his talent today.

He took a look at the limerick concept, and, perhaps in a mischievous moment, came up with one that did not rhyme at all!

There was an old man of St. Bees.
Who was stung in the arm by a wasp.
When asked, 'Does it hurt?'
He replied, 'No it doesn't;
I so glad that it wasn't a Hornet.'

of that whatever you will!